POWERPOINT
in easy steps

LL] **Stephen Copestake**

COMPUTER
STEP

In easy steps is an imprint of Computer Step
Southfield Road . Southam
Warwickshire CV33 OFB . England

Tel: 01926 817999 Fax: 01926 817005
http://www.computerstep.com

Reprinted 1998
First published 1997

Notice of Liability
Every effort has been made to ensure that this book contains accurate
and current information. However, Computer Step and the author shall
not be liable for any loss or damage suffered by readers as a result of
any information contained herein.

Trademarks
Microsoft® and Windows® are registered trademarks of Microsoft
Corporation. All other trademarks are acknowledged as belonging to
their respective companies.

Printed and bound in the United Kingdom

ISBN 1-874029-63-6

Contents

First steps

This section shows you how to launch PowerPoint and create new (or open existing) documents at the same time. You'll learn how to specify which toolbars display, how to work with differing document views and how to set Zoom levels. You'll also discover how to use PowerPoint's inbuilt HELP system (including the Office Assistant). Finally, you'll discover how to close PowerPoint.

Note that a basic familiarity with Windows is assumed throughout this book. For this reason, only features which are specific to PowerPoint are discussed.

Covers

Starting PowerPoint (1)

Launching PowerPoint is a multi-stage process.

First, click the Start button on the Windows Task Bar at the base of the screen:

Now do the following:

You can create a shortcut to run PowerPoint directly. See your Windows documentation for how to do this.

Click here

Task Bar

2 Click here

Starting PowerPoint (2)

PowerPoint now launches its Welcome screen. Do ONE of the following. Carry out step 1 below to create a new presentation with the AutoContent Wizard, or step 2 to create a new presentation based on a template. Alternatively, follow step 3 to create a blank slide show, or 4 to open one created earlier:

HANDY TIP

For more information on how to create new slide shows with:
• **the AutoContent Wizard**
• **templates see Section 2.**

Double-click here

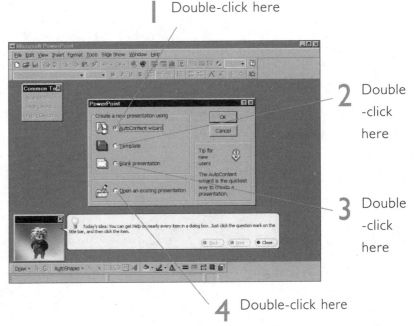

2 Double-click here

3 Double-click here

4 Double-click here

REMEMBER

To locate the file you want to open, click here; in the list, select the appropriate drive. Then double-click the relevant folder here:
Finally, carry out step 5.

If you carried out steps 1, 2 or 3, PowerPoint launches a variant of its main screen (see page 10 for more details). If, however, you followed step 4, the next dialog appears first. Perform step 5 below:

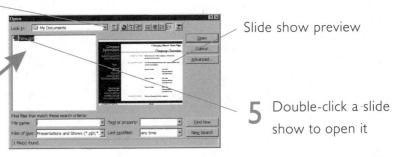

Slide show preview

5 Double-click a slide show to open it

The PowerPoint screen

When you've instructed PowerPoint to create a new presentation based on a template or with the help of the AutoContent Wizard (see page 8), or if you've elected to open an existing presentation, the final result will look something like this:

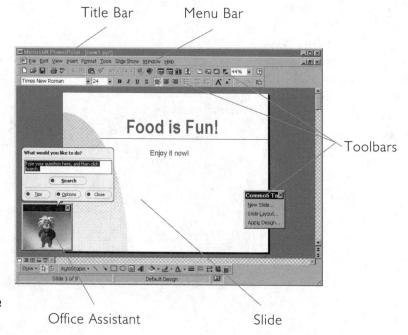

Title Bar   Menu Bar

Toolbars

Food is Fun!

Enjoy it now!

Office Assistant   Slide

REMEMBER

See pages 20-21 for how to use the Office Assistant in PowerPoint.

Note, however, that this is simply one 'view': Slide View. PowerPoint lets you interact with presentations in various ways. It does this by providing the following additional views:

*   Outline

*   Slide Sorter

*   Notes Page

See pages 16-17 later for more information.

Working with toolbars (1)

Toolbars are collections of icons. By clicking on the appropriate icon, you can launch a specific PowerPoint feature. Using toolbars saves you having to pull down menus and use dialogs.

PowerPoint comes with 11 toolbars. The most frequently used are:

Standard The most useful toolbar. Use this to open, save and print presentations, and to perform copy/cut and paste operations. Also used to:

   —   insert clip art

   —   insert new slides

   —   apply new slide layouts and designs

   —   change the slide zoom level

Formatting Use this to apply formatting options to slides and text

Drawing Use this to create shapes and lines, and to customise shape and line colour/formatting

Picture Use this to insert disk-based pictures into slides, and to apply formatting

Web Use this to go to World Wide Web sites instantly (providing you have a live Internet connection and modem), and to navigate through Web pages once you've arrived

Common Tasks Use this to insert new slides or apply new slide layouts and designs

HANDY TIP

Add tasks you perform frequently as icons in the Common Tasks toolbar.

For how to do this, see page 13.

Working with toolbars (2)

Specifying which toolbars display

You can have as many toolbars on-screen as you need.

Pull down the View menu and carry out the following steps:

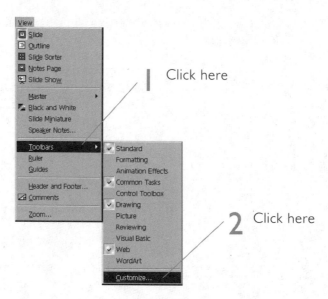

1 Click here

2 Click here

 HANDY TIP **Re step 4 – to hide or reveal a toolbar,** make sure you click the box to the left of the toolbar title:

A tick in the box means the selected toolbar is currently on-screen.

3 Ensure this tab is active

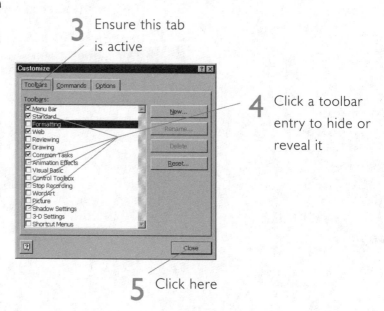

4 Click a toolbar entry to hide or reveal it

5 Click here

Working with toolbars (3)

Adding new icons to toolbars

Ensure the toolbar you want to add a new feature icon to is currently on screen (if it isn't, follow steps 1-5 on page 12). Pull down the View menu and do the following:

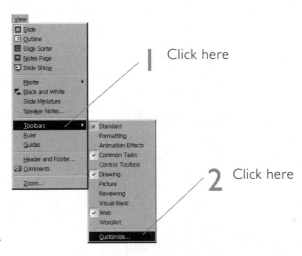

1 Click here

2 Click here

Re step 4 – toolbar commands are organised under overall Categories (feature sets).

3 Ensure this tab is active

To *delete* an existing toolbar icon, follow steps 1-3. Then drag the icon off the toolbar. (When you release the mouse button, it disappears.) Finally, carry out step 6.

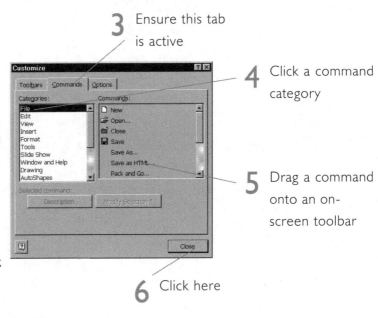

4 Click a command category

5 Drag a command onto an on-screen toolbar

6 Click here

Undo and Redo (1)

A very useful feature in PowerPoint is the ability to undo – or reverse – editing actions. Most editing actions can be undone with a couple of mouse clicks or a keyboard command. The main exceptions are:

You can even undo an undo. In PowerPoint, this is called 'redoing' – see 'Redoing an action' below.

- changing zoom levels

- opening or saving files

PowerPoint lets you specify the number of consecutive undos – you can opt for as many as 150.

Undoing an action
In the Standard toolbar, do the following:

Re step 2 – selecting an action which isn't at the top of the list automatically undoes earlier actions, too.

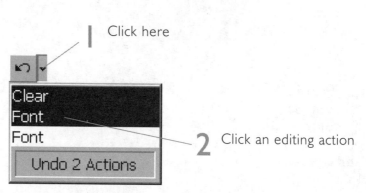

Click here

2 Click an editing action

You can use the following keyboard shortcuts:

Ctrl+Z   Undo
Ctry+Y   Redo

Redoing an action
In the Standard toolbar, do the following:

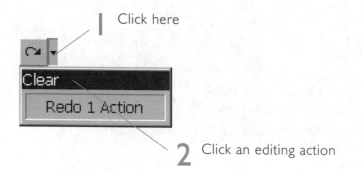

Click here

2 Click an editing action

Undo and Redo (2)

You can determine how many Undo levels PowerPoint supports.

Setting Undo levels

Pull down the Tools menu and do the following:

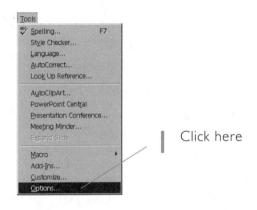

Click here

2 Ensure this tab is active

HANDY TIP

The default number of undos is 20.

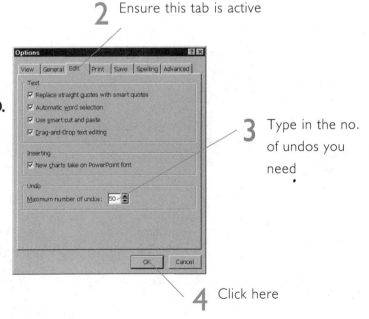

3 Type in the no. of undos you need

4 Click here

The slide views – an overview

These views are discussed in greater detail in later sections.

There are also various Master views – see Section 3 for how to use these.

The box at the top right-hand corner of the Outline view is the Slide Miniature. It provides a 'thumbnail' view of the slide you're working on in Outline view, so that you know when you've entered too much text. (To hide the Miniature, pull down the View menu and deselect Slide Miniature.)

PowerPoint has the following views:

Slide	displays each slide individually
Outline	shows the underlying textual structure of the presentation
Slide Sorter	shows all the slides as icons, so you can manipulate them more easily
Notes Page	shows each slide together with any speaker's notes

These are different ways of looking at your presentation. The best way to work with presentations is to use a combination of all four, as appropriate.

Switching to a view

Pull down the View menu and click Slide, Outline, Slide Sorter or Notes Page.

The four views are shown below:

Slide View

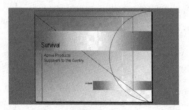

Outline View

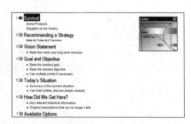

Slide Sorter View

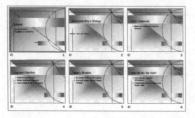

Notes Page View

Using the slide views

The following are some supplemental notes on how best to use the PowerPoint views.

Slide view

Slide view displays the current slide in its own window. Use Slide view when you want a detailed picture of a slide (for instance, when you amend any of the slide contents, or when you change the overall formatting).

To switch from slide to slide, you can press Page Up or Page Down as appropriate.

Outline view

If you're currently only working with the text in a given presentation, use Outline view. Outline view provides an overview of slide structure and content. The Slide Miniature – see the Handy Tip on page 16 – displays an accurate representation of the current slide for identification purposes.

Slide Sorter view

If you need to rearrange the order of slides, use Slide Sorter view. You can simply click on a slide and drag it to a new location (to move more than one slide, hold down one Shift key as you click on them, then drag). You can also copy a slide by holding down Ctrl instead of Shift as you drag.

To move to a specific slide in Slide Sorter view, double-click a slide icon; PowerPoint then displays the selected slide in Slide view.

Notes Page view

This view is an aid to the presenter rather than the viewer of the slide show. If you want to enter speaker's notes on a slide (for later printing), use Notes Page view.

In Notes Page view, the slide is displayed at a reduced size at the top of the page. Below this is a standard PowerPoint text object. For how to enter notes in this, see 'Working with speaker notes' on pages 122-123.

In Slide and Notes Page views, you can also use the vertical scroll bar to move to specific slides.

As you drag the scroll bar, PowerPoint displays a message telling you the number and title of the slide you're up to:

Slide: 1 of 9
Food is Fun!

Using Zoom

It's often useful to be able to inspect your presentations in close up; this is called 'zooming in'. Alternatively, sometimes taking an overview ('zooming out') is beneficial.

You can zoom in and out in any PowerPoint view (although the available options vary).

Setting the Zoom level

Pull down the View menu and do the following:

You can also use another method to set Zoom levels.
In the Standard toolbar, do the following:

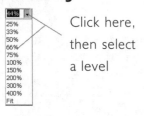

Click here, then select a level

Click here

If you want to use your own Zoom level (rather than a set magnification), type in the zoom % here:
Finally, carry out step 3.

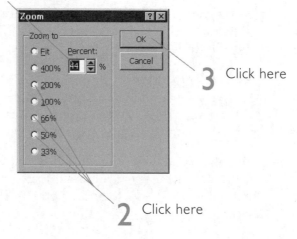

3 Click here

2 Click here

Using PowerPoint's HELP system

PowerPoint supports the standard Windows HELP system. For instance:

- moving the mouse pointer over toolbar buttons produces an explanatory HELP bubble:

Both of these features are called 'ScreenTips'.

- moving the mouse pointer over fields in dialogs, commands or screen areas and right-clicking produces a specific HELP box. Carry out the following procedure to activate this.

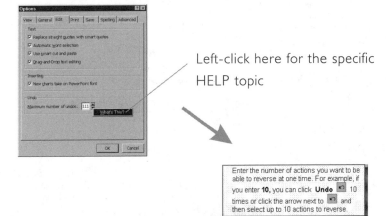

Left-click here for the specific HELP topic

To close down any HELP window when you've finished with it, simply press Esc.

Other standard Windows HELP features are also present; see your Windows documentation for how to use these.

PowerPoint also has one HELP feature which is unique to Microsoft Office 97 components: the Office Assistant. See the next topic for how to use PowerPoint's implementation of it.

Using the Office Assistant (1)

PowerPoint has a unique HELP feature, designed to make it much easier to become productive: the Office Assistant. The Office Assistant:

- answers questions directly. This is an especially useful feature for the reason that, normally when you invoke a program's HELP system, you know more or less the question you want to ask, or the topic on which you need information. If neither of these is true, however, PowerPoint's Office Assistant responds to Plain English questions and provides a choice of answers. For example, responses produced by entering 'What are ScreenTips?' include:

  — Show or hide toolbar ScreenTips

  — Ways to get assistance while you work

  — Show or hide shortcut tips keys in ScreenTips

- provides context-sensitive tips and HELP

The Office Assistant is animated. It can also change shape! To do this, click the Options button: In the dialog which appears, activate the Gallery tab. Click the Next button until the Assistant you want is displayed. Then click OK.

PowerPoint's Office Assistant (and HELP bubble), after it has just launched

If the Assistant HELP bubble isn't displayed, simply click anywhere in the Assistant.

Using the Office Assistant (2)

Launching the Office Assistant

By default, the Office Assistant displays automatically in PowerPoint. If it isn't currently on-screen, however, refer to the Standard toolbar and do the following:

Click here

Displaying tips

Ensure the Office Assistant is on-screen. Then do the following:

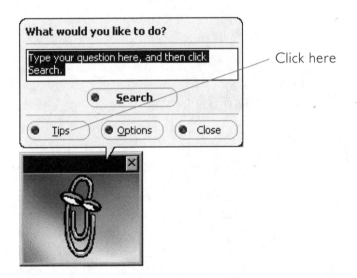

Click here

A context-sensitive tip appears. Carry out step 1 below when you've finished with it:

HANDY TIP

Click Next or Back (if available) to view another tip:

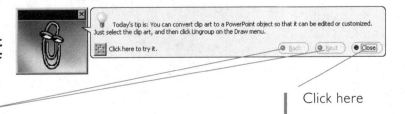

Click here

Closing down PowerPoint

To close down PowerPoint when you've finished using it, pull down the File menu and do the following:

Click here

If there are any unsaved changes to current presentations, PowerPoint now produces a special message.

Carry out step 1 below to save your work and then close PowerPoint. Alternatively, follow step 2 to close PowerPoint *without* saving your work:

2 Click here

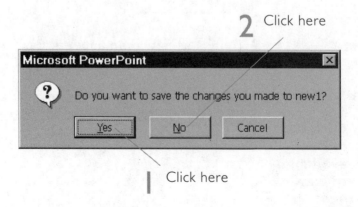

Click here

Creating a slide show

Use this section to acquire the basics of producing your own slide show in three ways. You'll learn how to apply new layouts to slides, and how to use existing text placeholders as a shortcut to text entry. You'll also create your own text boxes. Additionally, you'll format inserted text, work with slide outlines and then save your work to disk. Finally, you'll also discover how to save your slide shows to the Internet.

Covers

Creating new slide shows

 When you create slide shows based on templates, you can use a shortcut. If applicable, you can simply edit the text placeholders inserted when you apply AutoLayouts, rather than create your own text boxes. (See page 35 for how to edit existing placeholders, or page 36 for how to add and complete your own text boxes.)

PowerPoint lets you create a new presentation in the following ways (in descending order of ease of use):

- with the help of the AutoContent Wizard

- by basing it on a template, and creating each slide and its contents (apart from the background) manually

- by creating a blank presentation, and creating each slide and its contents (including the background) manually

The AutoContent Wizard is a high-powered yet easy to use shortcut to creating a slide show. It incorporates a question-and-answer system. You work through a series of dialogs, answering the appropriate questions and making the relevant choices. This is the easiest way to produce a slide show, but the results are nonetheless highly professional.

Templates – also known as boilerplates – are sample presentations, complete with the relevant formatting and/ or text. By basing a new slide show on a template, you automatically have access to these. Templates don't offer as many formatting choices as the AutoContent Wizard, but the results are equally as professional.

Slide shows created with the use of templates or the AutoContent Wizard can easily be amended subsequently.

Creating blank presentations is the simplest route; use this if you want to define the slide show components yourself from scratch. This is often not the most efficient or effective way to create new presentations. However, it isn't as onerous as might be imagined because PowerPoint lets you apply the following:

- pre-defined slide layouts (to individual slides)

- slide designs based on templates (see Section 3)

Using the AutoContent Wizard (1)

When you use the AutoContent wizard, you create a presentation which contains pre-defined content and design elements (although you can easily change as many of these as you want later). You can also choose from a large number of presentation types; these are organised under several headings (e.g. 'General', 'Corporate' and 'Projects') and are suitable for most purposes.

HANDY TIP

You also have the opportunity to launch the AutoContent Wizard as soon as you start PowerPoint – see page 9 in Section 1.

Launching the AutoContent Wizard

Pull down the File menu and click New. Now carry out the following steps:

Ensure this tab is active

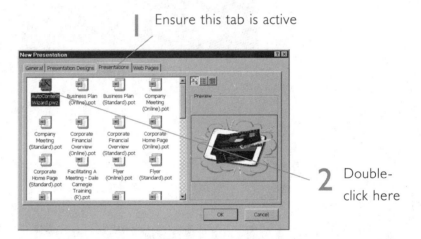

2 Double-click here

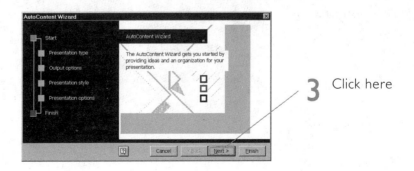

3 Click here

Using the AutoContent Wizard (2)

Now carry out the following steps:

Click a heading

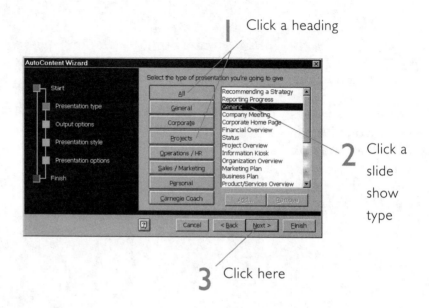

2 Click a slide show type

3 Click here

**Re step 4 –
click
'Internet,
kiosk' if
the presentation
you're creating will
be viewed without
your being present.**

4 Click here

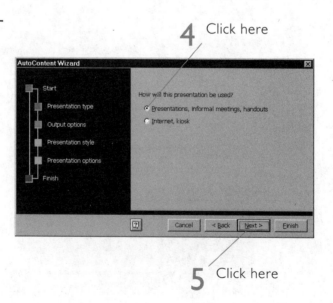

5 Click here

Using the AutoContent Wizard (3)

Carry out the following additional steps (only perform step 2 if you don't want to print handouts with your presentation):

Select an output type

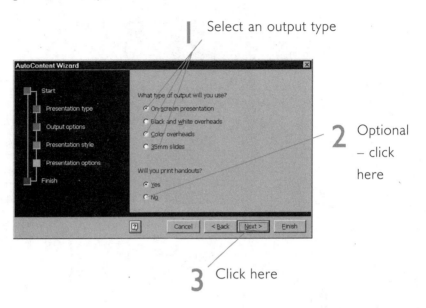

2 Optional – click here

3 Click here

4 Type in slide text

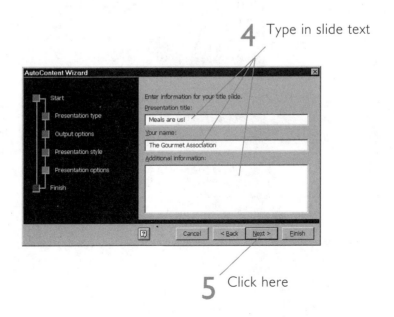

5 Click here

Using the AutoContent Wizard (4)

Now carry out the following steps:

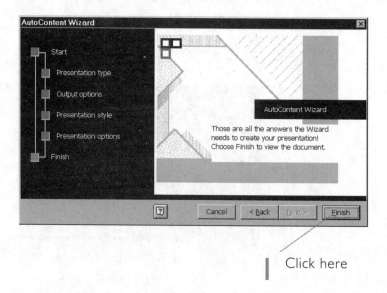

Click here

REMEMBER

Outline view is only one of several ways to interact with your slide shows – see pages 40-42.

PowerPoint now creates the new presentation:

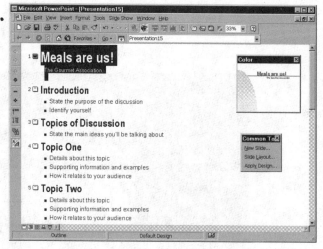

The final slide show, in Outline view (the default)

Using templates (1)

When you create a slide show with the help of a template, you:

1. Select a template

2. Apply a pre-defined layout

3. Type in the textual content

You also have the opportunity to create a new slide show based on a template as soon as you start PowerPoint – see page 9 in Section 1.

Step 1 applies to the overall presentation, while steps 2 and 3 have to be undertaken for every individual slide. This makes creating new presentations based on templates a slightly longer process than using the AutoContent Wizard. However, the end result is likely to be more personalised, and it's easier to have variations in individual style layout, if you need this.

Creating a new slide show based on a template

Pull down the File menu and do the following:

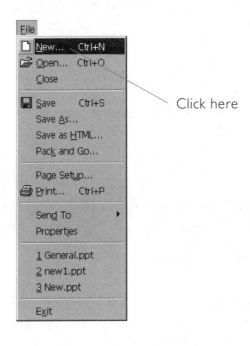

Click here

Using templates (2)

Now carry out the following additional steps:

Selected templates are previewed here:

I Ensure this tab is active

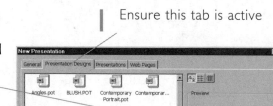

You can also use templates to create slide shows directly for the Internet.

In step 1, select the Presentations or Web Pages tabs. Double-click an Internet template. Now amend the template as appropriate (see later topics for how to do this). Save it in HTML format (see page 46), then send the completed files to your service provider.

2 Double-click a template

3 Double-click a layout

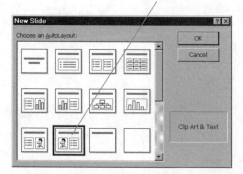

PowerPoint now creates the Title slide (slide number 1) for your presentation.

Using templates (3)

The Title slide for a new presentation is shown below:

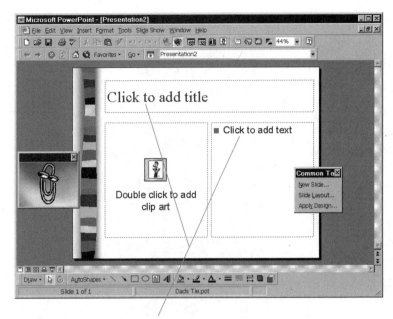

Text placeholders

Click in the text placeholders and type in the necessary text (for more information on how to do this, see page 35).

Creating additional slides

When you've finished filling in the Title slide, do the following in the Common Tasks toolbar to create a new slide based on the template you selected in step 2 on page 30:

When you've created new slides, add the necessary text in the supplied placeholders.

Click here

Now follow step 3 on page 30 to assign a slide layout.

Repeat this procedure under 'Creating additional slides' for as many new slides as you want to insert.

Creating blank slide shows (1)

To create a blank slide show, pull down the File menu and do the following:

 You also have the opportunity to create a new blank slide show as soon as you start PowerPoint – see page 9 in Section 1.

Click here

2 Ensure this tab is active

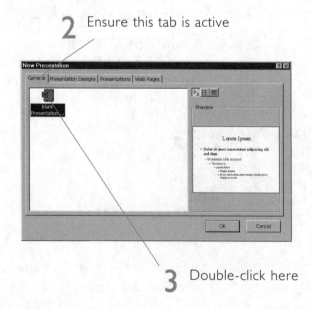

3 Double-click here

Creating blank slide shows (2)

Carry out the following additional step:

Double-click a layout

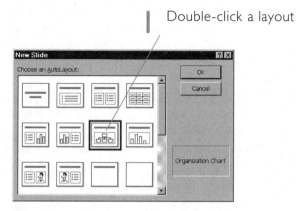

The resulting Title slide for a new blank presentation is shown below:

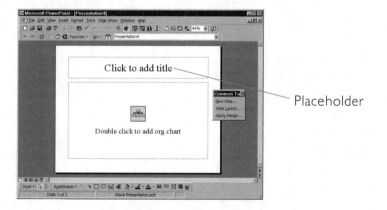

Placeholder

Click in the text placeholders and type in the necessary text (for more information on how to do this, see page 35).

When you've finished filling in the Title slide, follow the procedure under 'Creating additional slides' on page 31 to:

— add new slides

— assign layouts to them

— insert text in the relevant placeholders

Customising slide structure

Once you've created a slide show (using any of the methods discussed earlier), the easiest way to customise the basic format of a slide is to use AutoLayout. AutoLayout offers a selection of 24 layout structures and lets you apply your choice to a specific slide or group of slides. You can then amend the individual components (see later topics).

HANDY TIP

You can also customise slide shows by applying design templates – see Section 3.

Using AutoLayout

Make sure you're in Slide or Slide Sorter view (see page 16 for how to switch between views). If you're in Slide Sorter view, click the slide(s) you want to amend. Pull down the Format menu and click Slide Layout. Then do the following:

Click a slide format

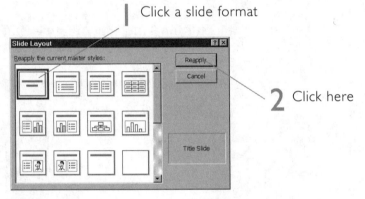

2 Click here

HANDY TIP

You can select more than one slide in Slide Sorter view by holding down one Shift key as you click on the slide icons.

Any slide components present before you applied the new format will still remain. However, they may need to be resized or moved. Look at the illustration below:

HANDY TIP

Standard mouse techniques can be used to reposition or rescale text objects in PowerPoint.

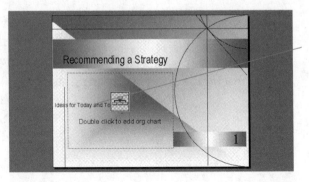

The imposition of the new format has meant that this text is now in the wrong location

Adding text to slides

When you create a new slide show (unless you create a blank presentation and choose to assign a blank AutoLayout to one or more slides), PowerPoint fills each slide with placeholders containing sample text. The idea is that you should replace this with your own text.

The illustration below shows a sample slide before customisation:

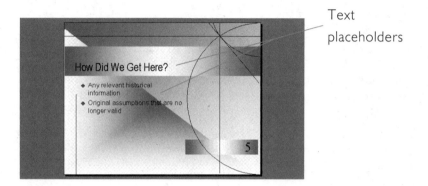

Text placeholders

To insert your own text, click in any text placeholder. PowerPoint displays a text entry box. Now do the following:

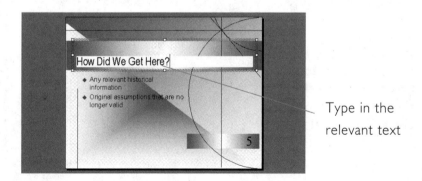

Type in the relevant text

Finally, click anywhere outside the placeholder to confirm the addition of the new text.

Inserting text boxes

If a slide contains no text placeholders, you can still insert text easily and conveniently by creating and inserting a text box.

Creating a text box

Refer to the Drawing toolbar. (If it isn't on-screen, see page 12 for how to make it display.) Do the following:

Click here

This way of defining a text box ensures that the text you enter subsequently is subject to wrap (i.e. surplus text automatically moves to the next line).

If you don't want this, simply follow step 1. Then click where you want the text to appear and begin typing immediately. PowerPoint extends the containing text box to ensure that the text stays on the original line.

Now move the mouse cursor over the slide. Position it at the point where you want the text box to begin. Drag to define the text box. Release the mouse button to confirm the operation.

Finally, type in the relevant text. Press Enter when you've finished.

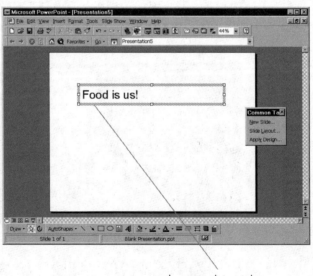

Inserted text box

Formatting text (1)

HANDY TIP

Text within slides is often automatically bulleted. If you want to add a bullet to text which isn't, however, click in the text. Pull down the Format menu and click Bullet. In the Bullet dialog, select a font in the Bullets from field. In the field below:

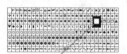

click the button you want to use. Finally, click OK.

HANDY TIP

Re step 6 – if none of the colours here are suitable, click More Colors. In the new dialog, click a colour in the polygon in the centre. Then click OK. Follow step 7 to apply the new colour.

You can carry out a variety of formatting enhancements on text. You can:

- change the font and/or type size
- apply a font style or effect
- apply a colour
- specify the alignment
- specify the line spacing

Font-based formatting

Click inside the relevant text object and select the text you want to format. Pull down the Format menu and click Font. Now carry out any of steps 1-6 below, as appropriate. Then follow step 7:

1 Click a new typeface

2 Type in a new point size

7 Click here

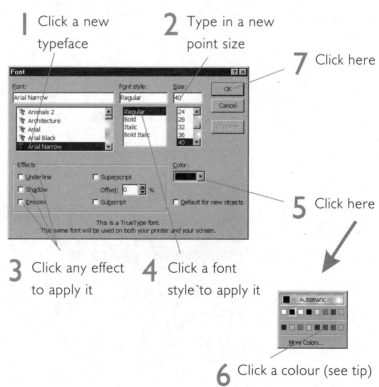

3 Click any effect to apply it

4 Click a font style to apply it

5 Click here

6 Click a colour (see tip)

Formatting text (2)

Changing text spacing

First, click inside the relevant text object and select the text whose spacing you want to amend. Pull down the Format menu and click Line Spacing. Now carry out any of steps 1-3 below, as appropriate. Then follow step 4.

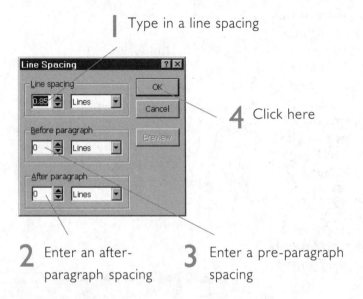

Type in a line spacing

4 Click here

2 Enter an after-paragraph spacing

3 Enter a pre-paragraph spacing

Changing text alignment

First, click inside the relevant text object and select the text whose alignment you want to amend. Pull down the Format menu and do the following:

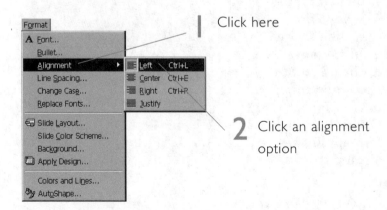

Click here

2 Click an alignment option

Formatting text (3)

Applying tabs

First, click inside the relevant text object. Ensure the ruler is on-screen. Now click in the ruler where you want the tab stop to appear:

HANDY TIP

If the ruler isn't currently visible, pull down the View menu and click Ruler.

Magnified view of inserted tab

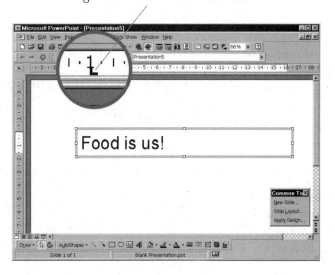

Food is us!

HANDY TIP

To delete a tab stop, simply drag it off the ruler.

Applying indents

First, click inside the relevant text object. Ensure the ruler is on-screen. Now do the following:

Drag this to revise the first-line indent

REMEMBER

Re step 2 – drag the square component:

Here

to revise the indent for *all* lines equally.

2 Drag this to revise the indent for all lines apart from the first

Working with slide outlines (1)

REMEMBER

You can have PowerPoint collect titles on specified slides and insert them into a new slide.
In Outline view, select the relevant slides (see page 42 for how to select more than 1). Then click the Summary Slide button:

in the Slide Sorter toolbar. PowerPoint inserts the new slide in front of the 1st selected slide.

Of the several views which PowerPoint supplies, Outline makes it easiest to work with your presentation as a whole.

In Outline view, no graphic elements display. Instead, only the titles and main text from each slide are visible. This is the most convenient way to organize and develop the content of your presentation.

In Outline view, you can:

* build presentation structures

* move entire slides from one position to another

* edit text entries

* hide or display text levels

Creating a presentation structure

First create a presentation, using any of the methods discussed earlier in this Section. Then pull down the View menu and click Outline. Now carry out step 1 below:

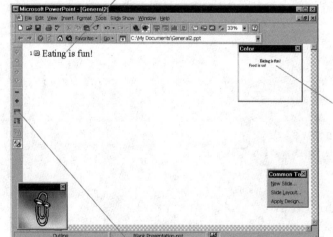

Type in title text and press Enter

Text you enter is mirrored in the Slide Miniature

Outline toolbar

REMEMBER

You can also expand bulleted paragraphs on one slide into title entries on new slides.
In any view apart from Notes Page, select the slide. Then pull down the Tools menu and click Expand Slide.

Working with slide outlines (2)

Now refer to the Outline toolbar and do the following:

Click here

'Demoting' a text entry moves it to a lower level.

When you press Enter in step 1 on page 40, PowerPoint creates a second title entry. The above action 'demotes' it to a bulleted entry. Do the following:

Type in bulleted text and press Enter

If you need to 'promote' a text entry (i.e. move it to a higher level), click in it. Then click this button in the Outline toolbar:

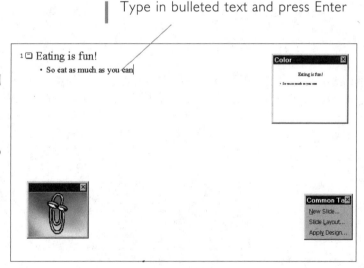

Repeat step 1 above as often as necessary. Finally, when you've finished creating text entries for the title slide, press Ctrl+Enter. This takes you to slide 2; use the techniques we've just discussed to add text to this. Repeat these procedures for as many slides as you want to include.

Working with slide outlines (3)

Moving slides

To reposition slides in Outline view, move the mouse pointer to the left of the text entry and left-click:

To select more than one text entry in Outline view, hold down one Shift key as you follow the procedures on the right.

Click here...

Eating is fun!
- So eat as much as you can
- Eat as often as you can
- Never take any prisoners
- Then eat some more

Or here

To edit a text entry, simply click in it. Then use standard Windows text editing techniques. Click outside the entry when you've finished.

Now drag the entry to a new level.

Hiding/displaying entries

An important feature of PowerPoint's Outline view is the ability to hide or reveal entries at will. This enables you to alternate between achieving a useful overview and viewing entries in detail.

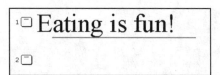

Eating is fun!

Here, the bulleted levels shown above have been collapsed...

The process of hiding entries is called 'collapsing'. Expanding is the reverse.

To hide or reveal a text entry, first click in it. Then refer to the Outline toolbar and do any of the following:

 Click here to collapse the entry

 Click here to expand the entry

Searching for text

PowerPoint lets you search for specific text within a slide show. For example, you can if you want have PowerPoint locate (successively) all instances of the word 'Food'.

You can also:

- limit the search to words which match the case of the text you specify (e.g. if you search for 'Food', PowerPoint will not go to slides which contain 'food' or 'FOOD')

- limit the search to whole words (e.g. if you search for 'food', PowerPoint will not find slides which contain 'foods')

Initiating a text search

Pull down the Edit menu and click Find. Now do the following:

Type in the text you want to find

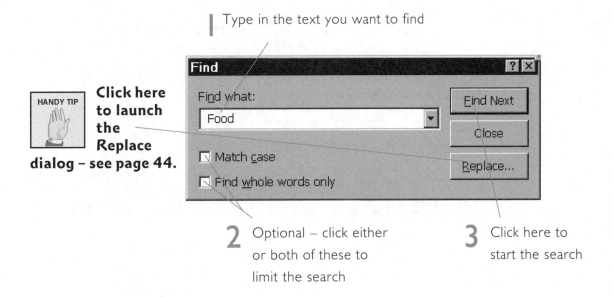

HANDY TIP **Click here to launch the Replace dialog – see page 44.**

2 Optional – click either or both of these to limit the search

3 Click here to start the search

Step 3 locates the first instance of the search text; repeat it to locate the next. And so on...

Replacing text

When you've located text, you can have PowerPoint replace it automatically (or one instance at a time) with the text of your choice.

When you undertake a find-and-replace operation, you can (as with find operations) make the search component case-specific, or limit it to whole-word matches. (See page 43 for illustrations of both of these restrictions.)

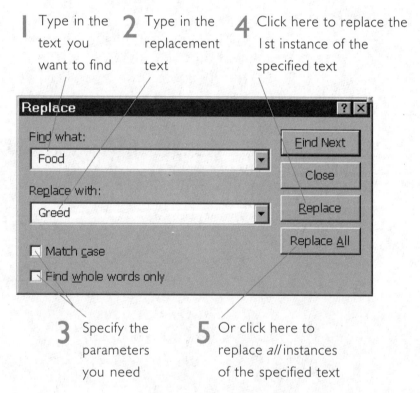
HANDY TIP

You can also launch the Replace dialog by clicking the Replace button in the Find dialog – see page 43.

Initiating a find-and-replace operation

First pull down the Edit menu and click Replace. Now follow steps 1 and 2 below. Carry out step 3, if appropriate. Finally, follow either step 4 or 5:

1 Type in the text you want to find

2 Type in the replacement text

4 Click here to replace the 1st instance of the specified text

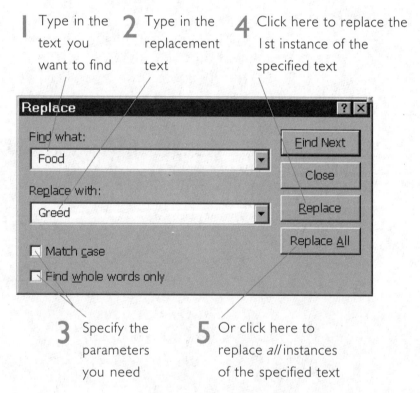

Replace	? X
Find what:	**Find Next**
Food	
	Close
Replace with:	
Greed	**Replace**
☐ Match case	Replace All
☐ Find whole words only	

3 Specify the parameters you need

5 Or click here to replace *all* instances of the specified text

Saving slide shows

It's important to save your work at frequent intervals, in order to avoid data loss in the event of a hardware fault or power interruption.

Saving a presentation for the first time

Pull down the File menu and click Save. Or press Ctrl+S. Now do the following (step 3 is optional):

2 Click here. In the drop-down list, click the drive you want to host the slide show

HANDY TIP

Re step 1 – by default, slide shows are saved in PowerPoint's own native format (extension: .PPT). However, if you want you can save them in a variety of additional formats. These include:

- **earlier versions of PowerPoint**
- **GIF (Graphics Interchange Format)**
- **JPEG**
Simply select the format you want in the list. (If you select GIF or JPEG, each slide – unless you specify otherwise – is saved as a separate picture file.)

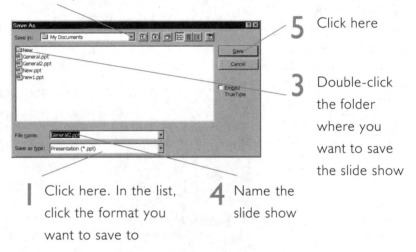

5 Click here

3 Double-click the folder where you want to save the slide show

1 Click here. In the list, click the format you want to save to

4 Name the slide show

Saving previously saved presentations

Pull down the File menu and click Save. Or press Ctrl+S. No dialog launches; instead, Office saves the latest version of your slide show to disk, overwriting the previous version.

Alternatively, refer to the Standard toolbar and do the following:

Click here

Saving to the Internet

REMEMBER

Re step 2 – to publish your slide shows on the Web, you must have access to the Internet (e.g. via a service provider), and you must have installed a modem. For help with step 2, consult your service provider. For more information on the Internet in general, read a companion volume: 'Internet UK in easy steps'.

You can save slide shows to any HTTP site on the World Wide Web. This is a two-stage process:

1.   saving your completed presentation in HTML (HyperText Markup Language) format

2.   sending copies of the HTML files to your service provider

Step 2 is outside the scope of this book.

Creating the relevant HTML files

Pull down the File menu and click Save as HTML. PowerPoint now launches a special Wizard. Do the following:

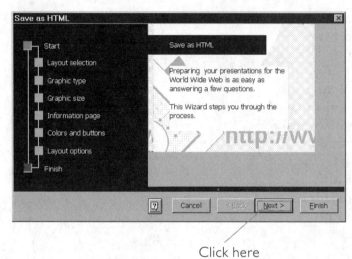

Click here

REMEMBER

You can use the Web toolbar to browse through or open any Web documents. For example: click ← to move backwards, → to move forwards. Click Favorites, Add to Favorites to add the current Web page to your list of often used sites...

Now complete the additional Wizard dialogs which appear. Finally, do the following:

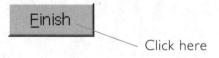

Click here

Slide design

Use this section to fine-tune the appearance of slides. You'll learn how to use the Slide and Title masters to ensure your presentations have a consistent look. You'll also discover how to apply and change colour schemes, and how to apply design templates, two additional techniques for achieving consistency. Finally, you'll amend slide headers and footers, and then save your presentation as a template for future use.

Covers

Customising slides – an overview (1)

PowerPoint provides several methods you can use to enhance slide appearance quickly and conveniently. You can:

- customise slide masters

For how to insert pictures into Master Slides, see Section 6.

- customise title masters

- apply a new colour scheme

- apply design templates

Slide Masters

Slide Masters are control slides which determine the format and position of *all* titles and text on slides (but see the Beware tip). You can also insert other objects – e.g. pictures – onto a Slide Master; when you do this, they're reproduced – unless you change this – on all slides after the first. In this way, if you want a picture – for instance, a company logo – to appear on every slide except the first, you can simply insert it on the Slide Master.

Slide Masters control text placing and formatting, but not content.

In other words, you can amend the appearance or position of text for all slides within a presentation, but not the text itself.

If you have specific text you want to appear on all slides apart from the first, insert a text box into the Slide Master. For how to do this, use the techniques discussed on page 36.

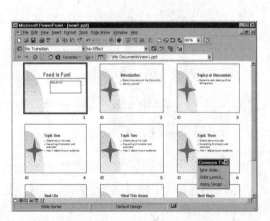

Here, a star has been added to the Slide Master; it appears on every slide apart from the first

Title Masters

Title Masters perform the same function as Slide Masters, but only in respect of the Title (first) slide together with any other slides you designate as title slides (you might do this with slides you want to announce distinct sections within the slide show).

Customising slides – an overview (2)

Colour schemes
Colour schemes are integrated collections of colours which are guaranteed to complement each other. Each colour scheme contains eight balanced colours which are automatically applied to slide elements such as:

- text

- background

- fill

You can apply colour schemes to individual slides, or to the whole of a presentation.

You can also create and use your own colour schemes.

Design templates
Design templates – otherwise known simply as designs – are collections of:

- Slide/Title masters

- colour schemes

- specific fonts which complement other elements in the design

When you apply a design template to a slide show (you can only do so en masse, not to specific slides), it takes precedence over the existing Slide Master and colour scheme. This means that when you create new slides, they automatically assume the characteristics of the new design template, irrespective of any AutoLayouts you may have applied previously.

Summary
Appropriate editing of Slide/Title Masters or the application of a new colour scheme represents a convenient technique for ensuring your slide show has a uniform appearance and/or content. Applying a new design template is a way of doing both at the same time.

Working with the Slide Master (1)

Editing the Slide Master is easy and convenient.

Launching the Slide Master
Pull down the View menu and do the following:

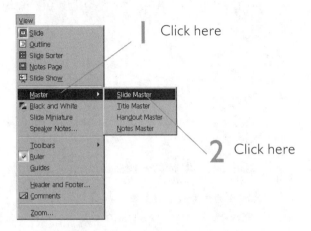

The illustration below shows the Slide Master for a presentation created with the help of a template:

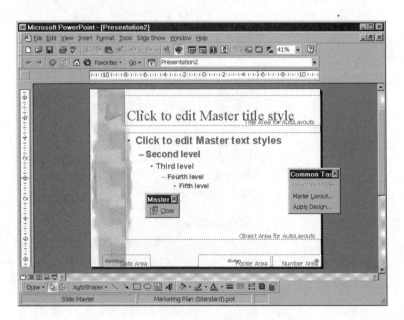

Working with the Slide Master (2)

Editing the Slide Master

Do any of the following:

 For how to format text within Slide Masters, use the techniques discussed on pages 37-39.

Click in a text entry, then apply any appropriate formatting enhancements

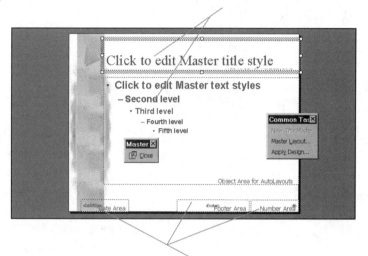

 For how to work with headers/ footers, see pages 60-61

 For how to insert pictures into Master Slides, see Section 6.

Click in a specialised text box, then apply any appropriate formatting enhancements

Closing the Slide Master

When you've finished with the Slide Master, do the following to return to the PowerPoint view you were using before you launched it:

Click here

Working with the Title Master (1)

Editing the Title Master is easy and convenient.

Launching the Title Master

Pull down the View menu and do the following:

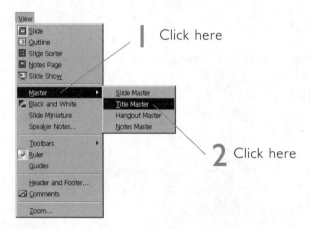

The illustration below shows the Title Master for a slide show created with the help of the AutoContent Wizard:

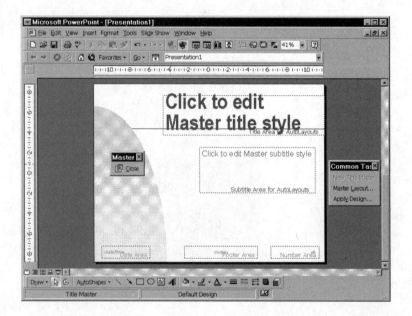

Working with the Title Master (2)

Editing the Title Master
Do any of the following:

For how to format text within Slide Masters, use the techniques discussed on pages 37-39.

Click in a text entry, then apply any appropriate formatting enhancements

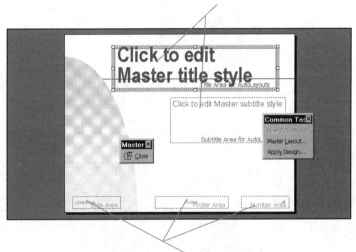

For how to work with headers/ footers, see pages 60-61.

Click in a specialised text box, then apply any appropriate formatting enhancements

Closing the Title Master

For how to insert pictures into Master Slides, see Section 6.

When you've finished with the Title Master, do the following to return to the PowerPoint view you were using before you launched it:

Click here

Applying colour schemes (1)

Applying a new colour scheme is a quick and effective way to give a presentation a new and consistent look.

Any PowerPoint presentation automatically has various colour schemes available to it (they're contained in the design template associated with the slide show).

Imposing a colour scheme

If you want to restrict the colour scheme to one or more slides, first do one of the following:

- In Slide view, go to the slide whose colour scheme you want to replace

- In Slide Sorter view, select one or more slides

Now pull down the Format menu and carry out the following action:

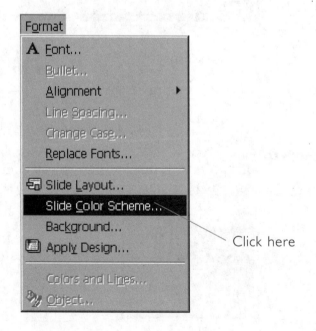

Click here

Applying colour schemes (2)

Now carry out step 1 below. If you want to apply the colour scheme to *all* slides within the active presentation, perform step 2. Alternatively, to apply it only to pre-selected slides, carry out step 3:

Click a colour scheme

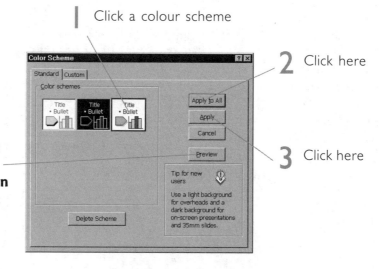

2 Click here

3 Click here

Click the Preview button on the right to see what your slides would look like after the application of the colour scheme.

PowerPoint now applies the selected colour scheme.

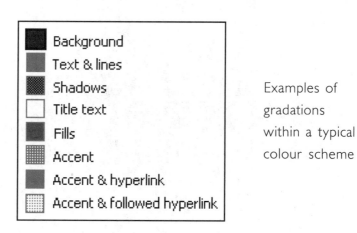

Examples of gradations within a typical colour scheme

Changing colours in a scheme (1)

If you need to, you can change individual colours within a colour scheme. When you do this, all slide objects associated with the colour are automatically updated.

In this way, colours in PowerPoint are similar to graphics styles within a word processor.

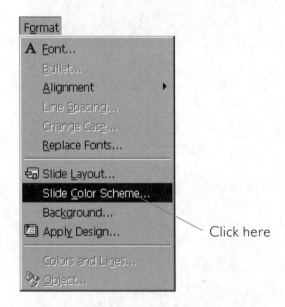

REMEMBER **Changing existing colour schemes like this is a way of creating your own – see also the Handy Tip on page 57.**

Amending a scheme colour

If you want to restrict the change to one or more slides, first do one of the following:

*   In Slide view, go to the slide whose colour scheme you want to replace

*   In Slide Sorter view, select one or more slides

Now pull down the Format menu and carry out the following:

Click here

Changing colours in a scheme (2)

Now carry out steps 1-5 below. Then, if you want to apply the colour scheme changes to *all* slides within the active presentation, perform step 6. Alternatively, to apply them only to pre-selected slides, carry out step 7:

REMEMBER
Click the Preview button on the right
to see what your slides would look like after the colour scheme changed.

HANDY TIP
To ensure that the colour changes
you've made are saved with the slide show, click the Add as Standard Scheme button before you carry out steps 5 or 6.

REMEMBER
If no colours are suitable, click the
Custom tab. Click a colour in the Colors box. Drag the slider on the right – ◄ – to adjust the brightness. Finally, carry out step 5.

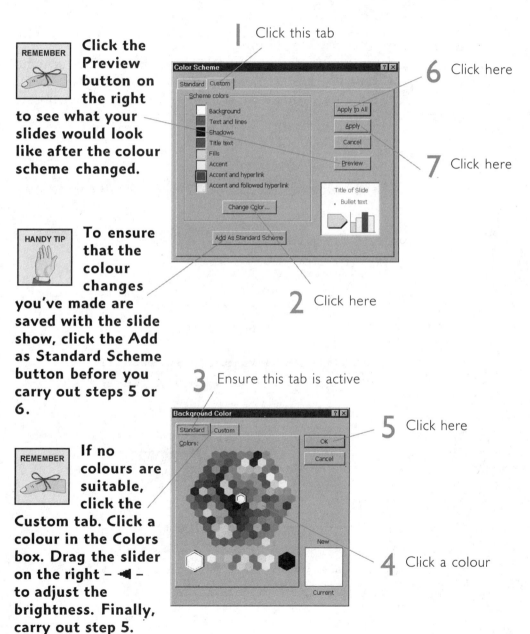

Click this tab

6 Click here

7 Click here

2 Click here

3 Ensure this tab is active

5 Click here

4 Click a colour

Colouring: a shortcut

PowerPoint offers a useful shortcut (the Format Painter) which enables you to copy a colour scheme:

- from one slide to another

- from one slide to multiple slides

For how to make the Standard toolbar visible, see page 12.

Copying colour schemes

In Slide Sorter view, select the slide whose colour scheme you want to transfer. Refer to the Standard toolbar; carry out step 1 for a single copy, or step 2 for multiple copies:

Click here

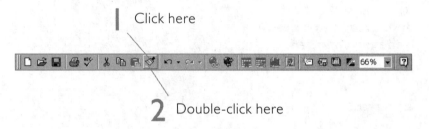

2 Double-click here

3 Click one or more slides, as appropriate

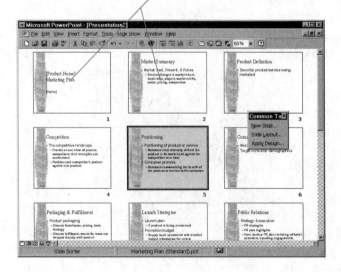

Applying design templates

When you apply a new design template to a presentation, you impose a potent combination of masters and colour schemes. For this reason, designs often represent the best and most convenient way to ensure presentations have an effective and consistent appearance.

Imposing a design

To apply a new design template to the active presentation, refer to the Common Tasks toolbar and do the following:

Re step 2 – the Apply Design dialog defaults to the folder which holds PowerPoint templates. If you want to use templates stored in a different drive/ folder combination, select it here.

Click here

2 Click here. In the drop-down list, click the appropriate drive/folder combination

You can also use slide shows themselves as the basis for a design. Click here: Select Presentations and Shows in the list. Then follow step 2 to select the relevant drive/ folder combination. Finally, carry out steps 3-4.

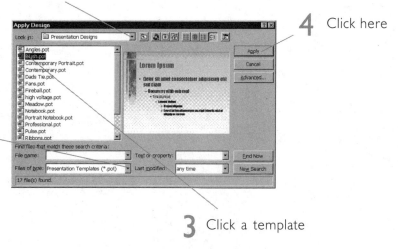

4 Click here

3 Click a template

Working with headers/footers (1)

Headers are text elements which appear at the top of each slide within a presentation; footers are elements which appear at the base of each slide.

Typically, you'll use headers and footers to display:

- the date and time of the presentation
- the slide or page number
- information specific to the current presentation

Once you've inserted information in the header and/or footer, you can change the appearance or position of the header and footer on your slides.

Using headers and footers

If you want to restrict your amendments to one or more slides, first do one of the following:

- In Slide view, go to the slide whose header you want to change
- In Slide Sorter view, select one or more slides

Now pull down the View menu and do the following:

To reposition or reformat header and footer elements, launch the Slide Master (see page 50 for how to do this). Select the element(s). Then do either or both of the following:
- **drag them to a new location**
- **apply new formatting characteristics (see pages 37-39)**

Click here

Working with headers/footers (2)

REMEMBER

Re step 1 – if you want to adjust the notes or handouts header/footer, click the Notes and Handouts tab. Then follow steps 2-7, as appropriate.
  Additionally, if you want a specific header, type it in the Header field. Click Page Number to have page numbers inserted in the header.

Now carry out step 1 below. If you don't want the date and time to display in the footer area, follow step 2. If you do want the date and time to display, omit step 2; follow step 3 instead. If you want the slide number to display in the footer, perform step 4. For specific slide information in the footer, carry out step 5.

Finally, if you want to apply the header/footer changes to *all* slides within the active presentation, perform step 6. Alternatively, to apply them only to pre-selected slides, carry out step 7:

HANDY TIP

Re step 3 – click here if you want the current date and time to be inserted *automatically.*

HANDY TIP

Click here if you don't want your changes to display on title slides.

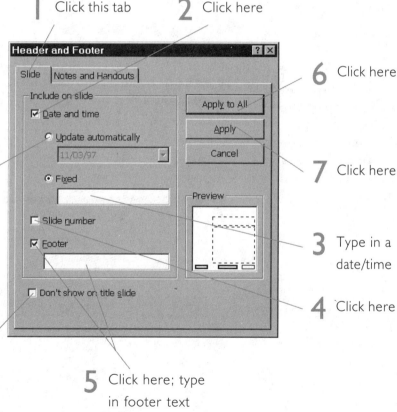

1 Click this tab

2 Click here

6 Click here

7 Click here

3 Type in a date/time

4 Click here

5 Click here; type in footer text

Saving your work as a template

If you want to create a template *without* **text or pictures, base a new slide show on an existing template. Make any formatting changes you want. Then follow steps 1-5 below.**

Be careful you don't save the original slide show after any deletions (unless you want this, of course).

PowerPoint lets you save slide shows you've created as templates. When you need to create a new presentation, you can then base it on the template (see pages 29-31 for how to do this). This technique can save you a lot of time and effort.

Templates you create using the procedures outlined below contain:

- masters

- colour schemes

- content (text and pictures)

Creating a template

Open the slide show you want to serve as the basis for a template. If necessary, delete text and pictures which you don't want to be included in the template. Then carry out the following steps:

2 Click here. In the drop-down list, click the drive you want to host the template

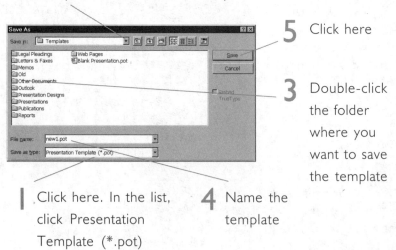

5 Click here

3 Double-click the folder where you want to save the template

1 Click here. In the list, click Presentation Template (*.pot)

4 Name the template

Using objects

Use this section to learn how to create and insert 'objects' (simple or complex graphic elements) in order to make your presentations more visually effective. You'll create lines, curves, rectangles/squares and ellipses/circles. Then you'll move on to AutoShapes, extraordinarily flexible graphics which are very easy to use.

Covers

Objects – an overview

HANDY TIP

You can use the following method to edit inserted objects (in addition to the techniques discussed in pages 75-82).

To edit a line, for example, click it; then drag to change the shape. Or double-click it to produce a dialog from which you can amend:

• the colour/fill
• the size
• the position
Finally, click OK.

HANDY TIP

All inserted objects can be moved with the use of standard Windows techniques.

You can add a variety of objects to your presentations:

- lines

- arrowed lines

- simple shapes (squares/rectangles and circles/ellipses)

- curves and freeform shapes

- a wide assortment of flexible shapes (known as AutoShapes)

The judicious inclusion of objects in your slide shows makes them more visual and can considerably enhance their effect.

AutoShapes are ready-made shapes you can define and manipulate with just a few mouse clicks. They're readily adjustable, and fall into several categories. The main ones are:

Action Buttons   Stars and Banners

Basic Shapes   Callouts

When you've inserted objects, you can manipulate them in several ways. You can:

- move them

- resize them

- rotate/flip them

- apply a colour/fill

- apply a shadow

- make them 3D

- (in the case of *complex* AutoShapes – see the Remember tip on page 65) convert them into other shapes

Creating lines (1)

Technically, all objects you insert in PowerPoint are AutoShapes. However, this book makes a functional distinction between simple objects (lines, curves etc.) and the more complex AutoShapes discussed in pages 75-82...

PowerPoint lets you create:

- straight lines

- single-arrowed lines

- double-arrowed lines

- curved lines

- freeform lines

Creating a straight line

First, ensure you're using Slide or Notes Pages view. Refer to the Drawing toolbar and do the following:

Click here

To constrain the new line to 15° increments, hold down one Shift key as you define it.

Now click where you want the line to begin and drag to define the line. Release the mouse button when you've finished.

To define the line outwards (to the left and right) from the starting point, hold down Ctrl as you drag.

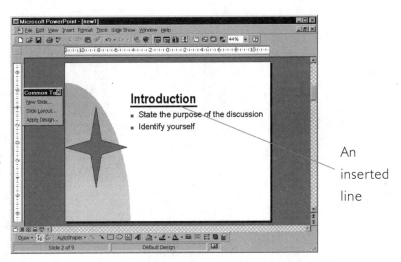

An inserted line

Creating lines (2)

Creating a single-arrowed line

First, ensure you're using Slide or Notes Pages view. Refer to the Drawing toolbar and do the following:

To constrain the new line to 15° increments, hold down one Shift key as you define it.

Click here

Now click where you want the arrowed line to begin and drag to define the line. Release the mouse button when you've finished.

To define the line outwards (to the left and right) from the starting point, hold down Ctrl as you drag.

Creating a double-arrowed line

First, ensure you're using Slide or Notes Pages view. Refer to the Drawing toolbar and do the following:

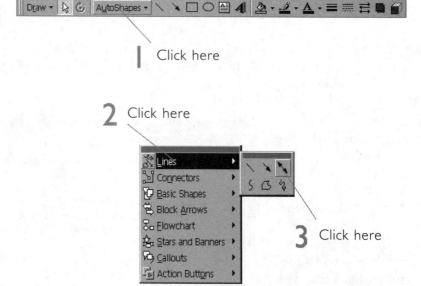

1 Click here

2 Click here

3 Click here

Now click where you want the arrowed line to begin and drag to define the line. Release the mouse button when you've finished.

Creating rectangles

Drawing a rectangle

First, ensure you're using Slide or Notes Pages view. Refer to the Drawing toolbar and do the following:

Click here

You use the same tool to create both rectangles and squares.

Now carry out these steps:

1. Place the mouse pointer where you want one corner of the rectangle to begin
2. Click and hold down the left mouse button
3. Drag to create the rectangle
4. Release the button

An alternative method

You may find it easier or more convenient to do the following.

Follow step 1 above. Then click in your slide where you want the rectangle to begin. PowerPoint inserts the following:

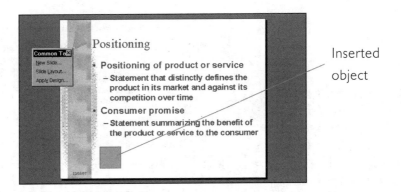

Inserted object

Now select and resize the object accordingly (for how to do this, see 'Resizing AutoShapes' on page 76).

Creating squares

Drawing a square

First, ensure you're using Slide or Notes Pages view. Refer to the Drawing toolbar and do the following:

Click here

Now carry out these steps:

1. Place the mouse pointer where you want one corner of the square to begin
2. Click and hold down the left mouse button
3. Hold down one Shift key
4. Drag to create the square
5. Release the button, then the Shift key

An alternative method

You may find it easier or more convenient to do the following.

Follow step 1 above. Then click in your slide where you want the square to begin. PowerPoint inserts a square:

Hold down one Shift key when you resize the square (if you don't, it becomes a rectangle).

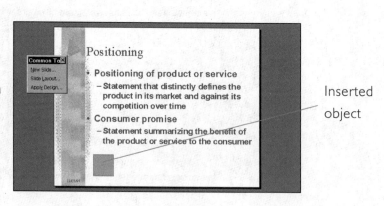

Inserted object

Now select and resize the object accordingly (for how to do this, see 'Resizing AutoShapes' on page 76).

Creating ellipses

Drawing an ellipse

First, ensure you're using Slide or Notes Pages view. Refer to the Drawing toolbar and do the following:

Click here

Now carry out these steps:

1. Place the mouse pointer where you want the ellipse to begin
2. Click and hold down the left mouse button
3. Drag to create the ellipse
4. Release the button

An alternative method

You may find it easier or more convenient to do the following.

Follow step 1 above. Then click in your slide where you want the ellipse to begin. PowerPoint inserts the following:

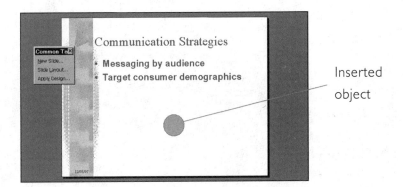

Inserted object

Now select and resize the object accordingly (for how to do this, see 'Resizing AutoShapes' on page 76).

Creating circles

Drawing a circle

First, ensure you're using Slide or Notes Pages view. Refer to the Drawing toolbar and do the following:

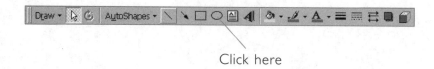

Click here

Now carry out these steps:

1. Place the mouse pointer where you want the circle to begin

2. Click and hold down the left mouse button

3. Hold down one Shift key

4. Drag to create the circle

5. Release the button, then the Shift key

An alternative method

You may find it easier or more convenient to do the following.

Follow step 1 above. Then click in your slide where you want the circle to begin. PowerPoint inserts a circle.

Hold down one Shift key when you resize the circle (if you don't, it becomes an ellipse).

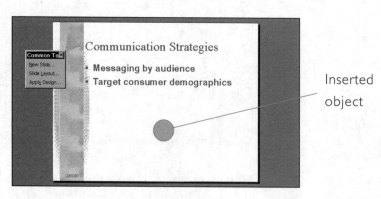

Inserted object

Now select and resize the object accordingly (for how to do this, see 'Resizing AutoShapes' on page 76).

Creating Bezier curves (1)

PowerPoint lets you create three types of curves

Bezier   provides great control and accuracy

Freeform   freehand curves without jagged edges

Scribble   a lifelike imitation of freehand drawing

Defining Bezier curves

If you need to create curves in your presentations, this is the technique you'll normally use. In effect, you provide PowerPoint with details of where two points should be placed and it creates the appropriate curve between them, smoothly and efficiently.

First, ensure you're using Slide or Notes Pages view. Refer to the Drawing toolbar and do the following:

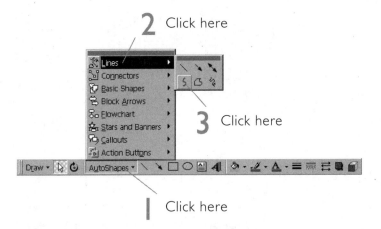

Now carry out these steps:

1.   Place the mouse pointer where you want the curve to begin

2.   Click and hold down the left mouse button

3.   Drag to create the first curve coordinate

Creating Bezier curves (2)

The first stage of your curve should look something like this:

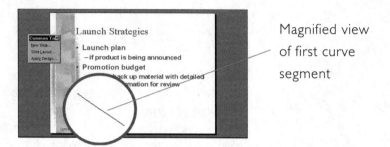

Magnified view of first curve segment

Now left-click once. Move the mouse pointer to define the second curve coordinate. PowerPoint creates the curve:

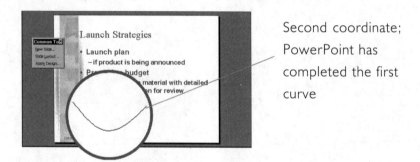

Second coordinate; PowerPoint has completed the first curve

Repeat the above procedure for as many curves as you want to define.

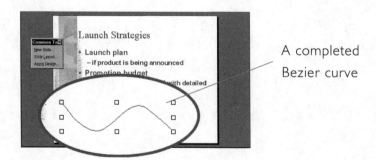

A completed Bezier curve

Creating freehand curves (1)

Drawing freehand curves

Drawing freehand curves is one of PowerPoint's least user-friendly operations, in the sense that using it effectively requires some artistic ability. In fact, it's probably the feature you'll use least of all. However, freehand drawing in PowerPoint can create highly original effects. Think of it like using a pencil, or an Etch-a-Sketch.

First, ensure you're using Slide or Notes Pages view. Refer to the Drawing toolbar and do the following:

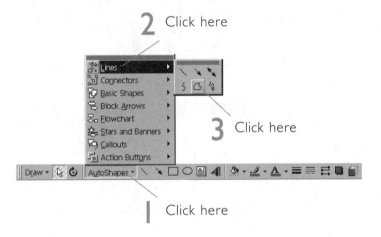

Now carry out these steps:

1. Place the mouse pointer where you want your curve to start.

2. Hold down the left mouse button.

3. Drag out the curves you need.

4. Release the mouse button when you've finished.

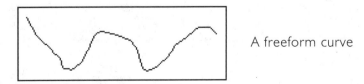

A freeform curve

Creating freehand curves (2)

Drawing freehand curves with Scribble

Using the Scribble tool requires even more artistic ability
that drawing freehand curves.

First, ensure you're using Slide or Notes Pages view. Refer
to the Drawing toolbar and do the following:

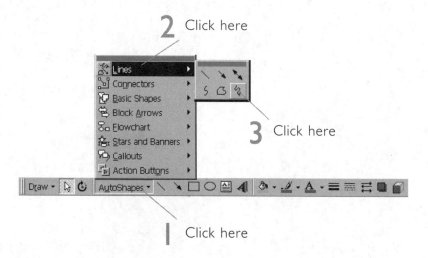

Now carry out these steps:

1. Place the mouse pointer where you want your curve to
    start.

2. Hold down the left mouse button.

3. Drag out the curves you need.

4. Release the mouse button when you've finished.

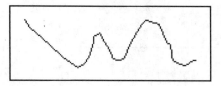

A curve created with
the Scribble tool

Using AutoShapes (1)

 You can easily add text to inserted AutoShapes.
Right-click the AutoShape. In the menu, click Add Text. The insertion point appears in the centre; type in the text. Click outside the AutoShape.

AutoShapes represent an extraordinarily flexible and easy-to-use way to insert a wide variety of shapes into your presentations. Once inserted, they can be:

- resized
- rotated/flipped
- coloured/filled
- converted into other shapes

Inserting an AutoShape

First, ensure you're using Slide or Notes Pages view. Refer to the Drawing toolbar and do the following:

 Text which has been inserted into an AutoShape becomes an integral part of it: any changes you make to the AutoShape also affect the text.

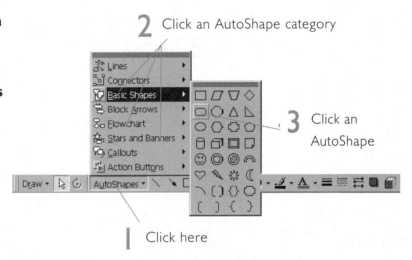

Now carry out these steps:

 You can use a shortcut to insert AutoShapes.
Follow step 1. Then simply click where you want the AutoShape inserted. Now resize it appropriately – see page 76.

1. Place the mouse pointer where you want your AutoShape to start.

2. Hold down the left mouse button.

3. Drag out the shape.

4. Release the mouse button when you've finished.

Using AutoShapes (2)

Resizing AutoShapes

In Slide or Notes Pages view, select the AutoShape. Now do the following:

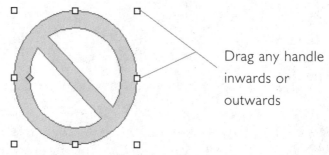

Drag any handle inwards or outwards

HANDY TIP

You can use these techniques with *any* drawing object created in PowerPoint.

Rotating AutoShapes

In Slide or Notes Pages view, select the AutoShape. Now refer to the Drawing toolbar and do the following:

HANDY TIP

To rotate in 90° stages, don't follow steps 1 or 2. Instead, click here:
In the menu, click Rotate or Flip. In the sub-menu, click Rotate Left or Rotate Right.

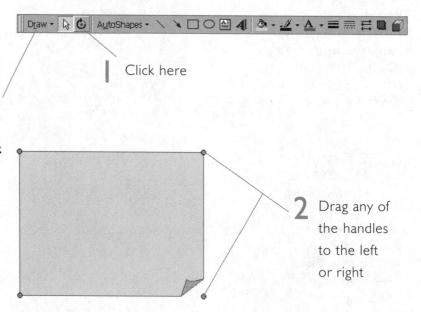

Click here

2 Drag any of the handles to the left or right

Using AutoShapes (3)

Flipping AutoShapes

In Slide or Notes Pages view, select the AutoShape. Refer to the Drawing toolbar and do the following:

You can use this technique with *any* drawing object created in PowerPoint.

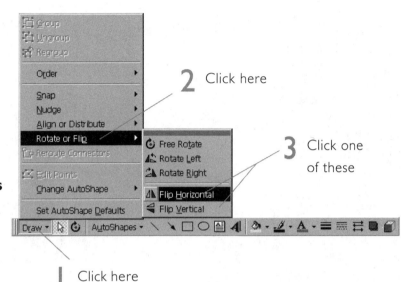

2 Click here

3 Click one of these

Click here

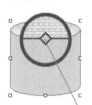

Most AutoShapes have a special handle:

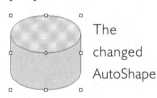

Magnified view of AutoShape handle

Dragging on this changes the AutoShape's properties:

The changed AutoShape

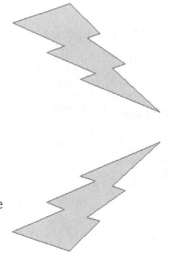

An AutoShape object

The same object after vertical flip

Using AutoShapes (4)

Applying fills to AutoShapes

In Slide or Notes Pages view, select the AutoShape. Now do the following:

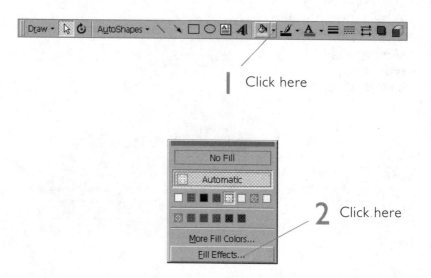

You can use this technique with *any* drawing object created in PowerPoint.

I Click here

2 Click here

3 Click a tab

Re step 4 – the available options depend on which tab you've selected in step 3.

5 Click here

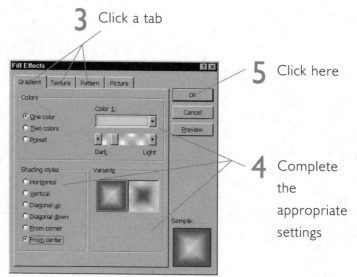

4 Complete the appropriate settings

Using AutoShapes (5)

Amending fill colours

In Slide or Notes Pages view, select the AutoShape. Refer to the Drawing toolbar. Carry out step 1. If the available colours are suitable, perform step 2. If not, carry out steps 3 and 4 instead.

 HANDY TIP **You can use these techniques with *any* drawing object created in PowerPoint.**

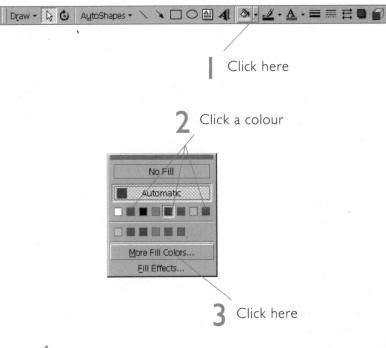

| Click here

2 Click a colour

3 Click here

 REMEMBER **Re step 4 – if you want to define your own colour, click the Custom tab instead. Click a colour in the Colors box. Drag the slider on the right – ◀ -- to adjust the brightness. Finally, omit step 5; instead, click OK.**

4 Click here

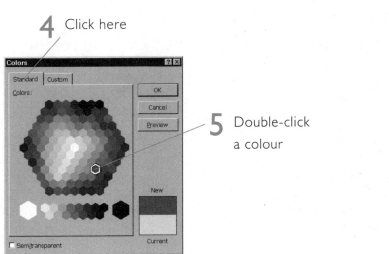

5 Double-click a colour

Using AutoShapes (6)

Applying shadow to AutoShapes

In Slide or Notes Pages view, select the AutoShape. Refer to the Drawing toolbar and do the following:

You can use these techniques with *any* drawing object created in PowerPoint.

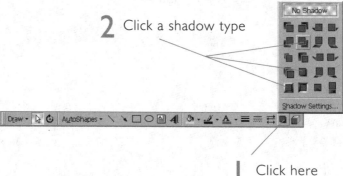

2 Click a shadow type

Click here

To vary the shadow colour, select the object. Follow step 1. In the drop-down Shadow list, click the Shadow Settings button. The Shadow Settings toolbar launches. Do the following:

Click here

In the drop-down list, click a colour. Or click More Shadow Colors in the list, then carry out steps 4-5 on page 79.

An AutoShape object

The object complete with shadow

Using AutoShapes (7)

Applying 3D to AutoShapes

In Slide or Notes Pages view, select the AutoShape. Refer to the Drawing toolbar and do the following:

You can use these techniques with *any* drawing object created in PowerPoint.

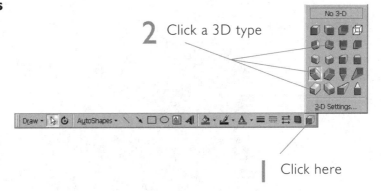

2 Click a 3D type

Click here

To vary the 3D colour, select the object. Follow step 1. In the drop-down 3D list, click the 3-D Settings button. The 3-D Settings toolbar launches. Do the following:

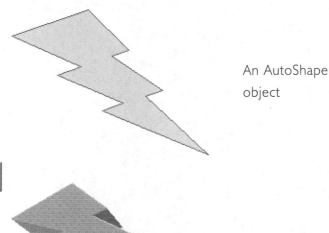

An AutoShape object

Click here

In the drop-down list, click a colour. Or click More 3-D Colors in the list, then carry out steps 4-5 on page 79.

The object in 3D

Using AutoShapes (8)

Converting AutoShapes

In Slide or Notes Pages view, select the AutoShape. Refer to the Drawing toolbar and do the following:

HANDY TIP **You can use this technique with *any* drawing object created in PowerPoint.**

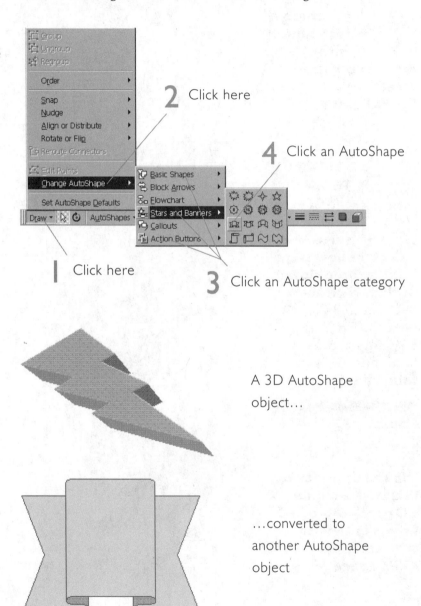

2 Click here

4 Click an AutoShape

I Click here

3 Click an AutoShape category

A 3D AutoShape object...

...converted to another AutoShape object

Using charts

Charts improve slide impact. Use this section to learn how to create and insert new charts. You can do this from within PowerPoint itself with the help of the Datasheet (an inbuilt mini-spreadsheet), or you can base charts on imported data in a variety of external formats. Once you've created charts, you'll learn how to allocate a new chart type. Finally, you'll discover how to reformat the various chart components.

Covers

Charts – an overview

PowerPoint makes it easy to insert charts into your presentations. You can do this in two ways:

- by double-clicking chart placeholders (if the slide you're inserting the chart into has had the appropriate AutoLayout applied to it)

- by using a menu route

When you insert a chart, the data on which it's based is displayed in a special window called the Datasheet. The Datasheet can be regarded as a mini version of a typical spreadsheet, and contains sample data which you can easily amend.

REMEMBER

When you create or work with charts in PowerPoint, you're actually running a separate program: Microsoft Graph. Graph runs seamlessly within the PowerPoint environment.

Once you've inserted a chart, you can:

- edit the data

- reformat the Datasheet

- import data from a variety of external sources, including Microsoft Excel files

- apply a new chart type/sub-type

- reformat chart objects

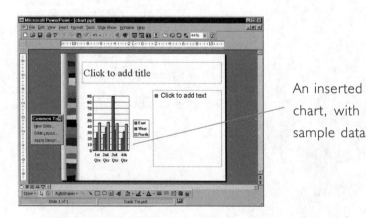

An inserted chart, with sample data

Chart components

PowerPoint offers 14 overall chart types. There are also numerous sub-types (variants on a theme). In addition, PowerPoint charts are very customisable: they can contain a wide variety of features/components. The illustration below shows the main ones:

Most charts do not contain all of these elements (they would simply become too cluttered); they're shown here for illustration purposes.

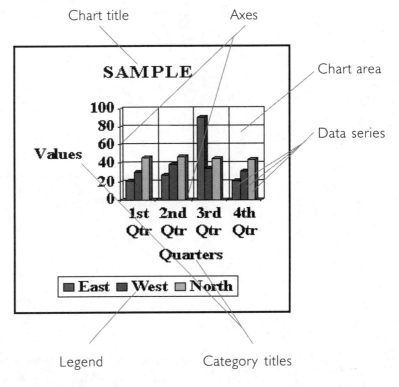

Chart title   Axes

SAMPLE

Chart area

Data series

Values

1st 2nd 3rd 4th
Qtr Qtr Qtr Qtr

Quarters

■ East ■ West ■ North

Legend   Category titles

A data series is a group of related values taken from a Datasheet row (horizontal) or column (vertical). In this chart, there are three: East, West and North. (For more information on the use of the Datasheet, see pages 88-89.)

The distinctions listed here between the X, Y and Z axes are sometimes blurred.

Axes are lines which border the chart area; chart values are measured against axes. In most charts, the Y (Value) axis is vertical, while the X (Category) axis is horizontal.

Some charts also have a Z (Time) axis which allows values to be related to time.

Inserting charts (1)

Inserting charts – the placeholder route

In Slide view, display the slide into which you want to insert the chart. Carry out the following steps:

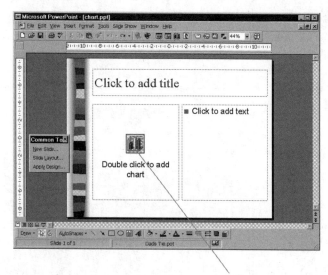

Double-click here

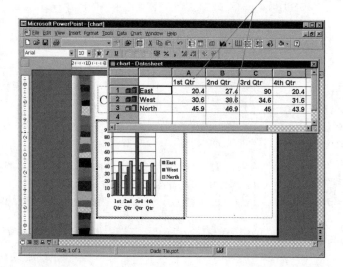

2 Complete the Datasheet, then click anywhere in the slide

HANDY TIP **Re step 2 – for how to complete the Datasheet, see page 88.**

Inserting charts (2)

Inserting charts – the menu route

In Slide view, display the slide into which you want to insert the chart. Carry out the following steps:

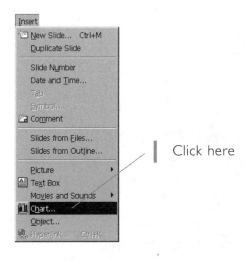

Click here

HANDY TIP **Re step 2 – for how to complete the Datasheet, see page 88.**

2 Complete the Datasheet, then click anywhere in the slide

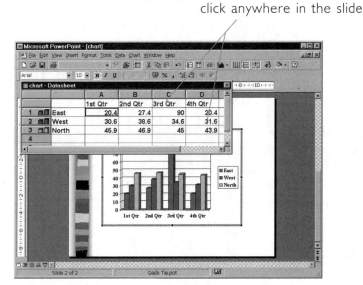

Editing chart data

After you've created a chart, and irrespective of the way you created it, you can revise the data on which it's based. PowerPoint makes this process easy and convenient.

Amending data

Right-click over the chart you want to amend. Do the following:

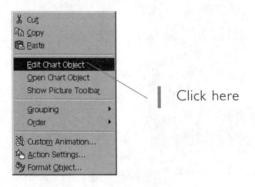

Click here

PowerPoint launches the Datasheet. Perform any of the following steps:

Cells

2 Amend the axis titles

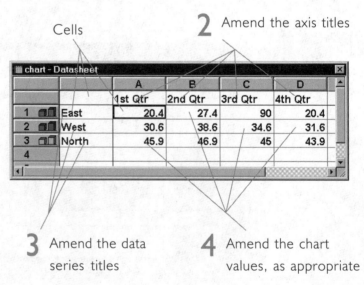

		A	B	C	D
		1st Qtr	2nd Qtr	3rd Qtr	4th Qtr
1	East	20.4	27.4	90	20.4
2	West	30.6	38.6	34.6	31.6
3	North	45.9	46.9	45	43.9
4					

HANDY TIP

If you want to hide the Datasheet while leaving the chart active, pull down the View menu and click Datasheet.

3 Amend the data series titles

4 Amend the chart values, as appropriate

When you've finished, click outside the Datasheet.

Reformatting the Datasheet

BEWARE

Formatting changes you make to the Datasheet have no effect on the way your data is represented in the associated chart.

To a limited extent, you can customise how the Datasheet presents information. You can:

- change the typeface/type size

- specify how numbers display (e.g. you can set the number of decimal points)

Applying a typeface/type size

Double-click the relevant chart. If the Datasheet isn't visible, pull down the View menu and click Datasheet. Pull down the Format menu and click Font. Carry out the following:

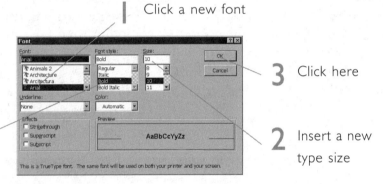

Click a new font

HANDY TIP

You can also embolden and/or italicise text.
  Click one of the options here: before you carry out step 4.

3 Click here

2 Insert a new type size

Applying a number format

Double-click the relevant chart. If the Datasheet isn't visible, pull down the View menu and click Datasheet. Pull down the Format menu and click Number. Carry out the following:

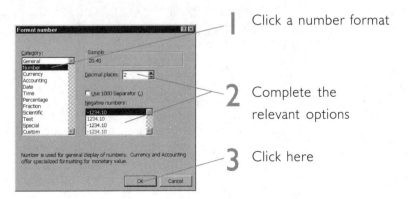

REMEMBER

Re step 2 – the available options depend on the number format chosen in step 1.

Click a number format

2 Complete the relevant options

3 Click here

Importing data (1)

Most database and spreadsheet programs readily export data as text files.

There are different types. For example, units of data can be differentiated by:
• commas
• tab marks
• spaces
PowerPoint imports them all equally well.

You can have PowerPoint create charts from third-party data. You can import:

*   Microsoft Excel files

*   Lotus 1-2-3 files

*   text files, also known as 'delimited' or CSV (Comma Separated Value) files

Importing Excel data

Within Slide view, go to the slide in which you want the new chart created. Pull down the Insert menu and click Chart; PowerPoint inserts a new chart with sample data and launches the Datasheet. If you want the inserted data to begin in any cell other than the upper left, click it. Pull down the Edit menu and click Import File. Now carry out the following:

2 Click here. In the drop-down list, click the drive which hosts the Excel file

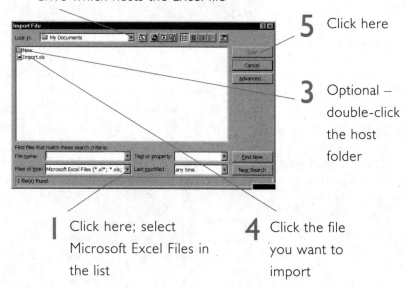

5 Click here

3 Optional – double-click the host folder

Click here; select Microsoft Excel Files in the list

4 Click the file you want to import

Importing data (2)

PowerPoint now launches a special dialog.

Carry out the following steps:

Re step 1 – type in the start and end cell addresses, separated by a colon.

For instance, to chart only cells H8 to J11, type:

H8:J11

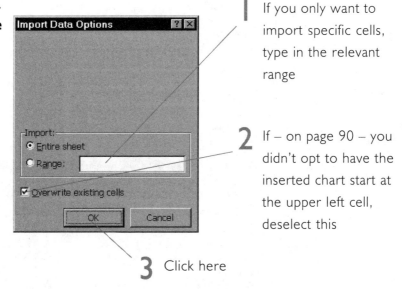

1 If you only want to import specific cells, type in the relevant range

2 If – on page 90 – you didn't opt to have the inserted chart start at the upper left cell, deselect this

3 Click here

PowerPoint now creates a new chart based on the imported data.

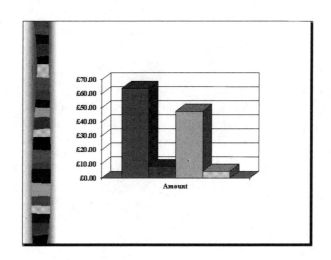

A (simple) inserted chart based on Excel data

Importing data (3)

Importing 1-2-3 data

Within Slide view, go to the slide in which you want the new chart created. Pull down the Insert menu and click Chart; PowerPoint inserts a new chart with sample data and launches the Datasheet. If you want the inserted data to begin in any cell other than the upper left, click it. Pull down the Edit menu and click Import File. Now carry out the following:

2 Click here. In the drop-down list, click the drive which hosts the Excel file

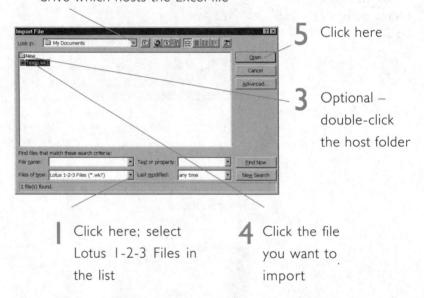

5 Click here

3 Optional – double-click the host folder

| Click here; select Lotus 1-2-3 Files in the list

4 Click the file you want to import

In the case of Lotus 1-2-3 files, no further dialog launches. This means that you can only import the *whole* of a 1-2-3 file: you can't specify a cell range for inclusion within PowerPoint.

If you only want to import a cell range, create a copy of the relevant 1-2-3 file and delete the unwanted cells within 1-2-3 itself . Then follow steps 1-5 to import the restricted file.

Importing data (4)

Importing data in text files

Within Slide view, go to the slide in which you want the new chart created. Pull down the Insert menu and click Chart; PowerPoint inserts a new chart with sample data and launches the Datasheet. If you want the inserted data to begin in any cell other than the upper left, click it. Pull down the Edit menu and click Import File. Now carry out the following:

2 Click here. In the drop-down list, click the drive which hosts the Excel file

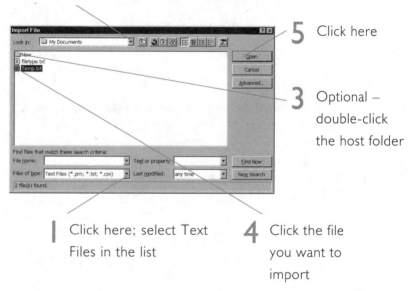

5 Click here

3 Optional – double-click the host folder

Click here; select Text Files in the list

4 Click the file you want to import

PowerPoint now launches a 3-stage wizard.

Complete each stage as per the instructions on page 94. However, you should note the following:

- PowerPoint auto-completes most of the settings in the wizards (and previews changes)

- only change these automatic settings if they're not suitable

Importing data (5)

Completing the Text Import Wizard

Carry out the following steps:

Re steps 1-2, 4 and 6-7 – only change these settings if the Data Preview section (see the tip below) reveals that they're not suitable.

I Optional – select another file type

2 Optional – specify where the import begins

3 Click here

The results of any manual changes you make are shown in the Data Preview section:

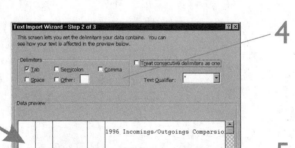

4 Optional – in this section, specify a new text delimiter

5 Click here

7 Optional – click a data format

Repeat steps 6-7 for as many columns as you need to amend. Then carry out step 8.

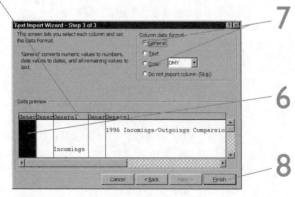

6 Optional – click a column entry

8 Click here

Applying a new chart type (1)

After you've inserted a chart, you can change the chart type. There are 14 overall chart types. Some of the most commonly used are:

- Bar

- Pie

- Line

- Area

All of the 14 types have a minimum of 2 sub-types associated with them; most have 6 or more. Often, the available sub-types include 3D alternatives:

A 'Lines' sub-type

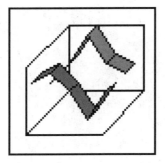

A 'Lines' 3D sub-type

PowerPoint makes switching between types and sub-types easy and convenient.

Applying a new chart type (2)

Changing chart types

Double-click the relevant chart. Then pull down the Chart menu and do the following:

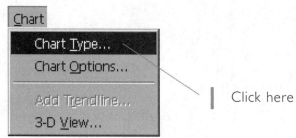

Click here

If you want, you can apply *customised* **chart types. These are professionally designed formats which also incorporate:**
- **colours**
- **patterns**
- **legends and other chart components**

To apply a custom type, don't follow step 2. Instead, activate the Custom Types tab. Then carry out steps 3-5.

A custom chart type:

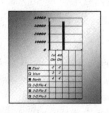

2 Ensure this tab is active

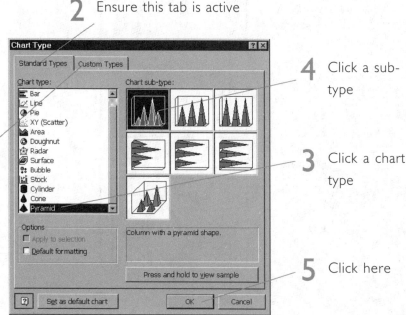

4 Click a sub-type

3 Click a chart type

5 Click here

Formatting chart components (1)

After you've inserted a chart, you can easily vary the formatting. You can select specific chart objects and:

The precise formatting changes you can carry out depend on the object selected. For instance, you can only apply a new typeface/type size to text objects.

- apply a colour

- apply a texture/pattern as a fill

- change the line width/border style

- apply a new typeface/type size

Applying a colour

In Slide view, go to the slide which hosts the chart you want to amend. Double-click the chart. Now do the following:

Re step 1 – here, one of the three data series has been selected.

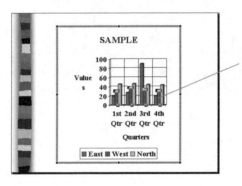

Double-click the component you want to recolour

2 Ensure this tab is active

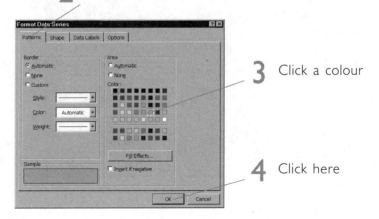

3 Click a colour

4 Click here

Formatting chart components (2)

Applying a fill

In Slide view, go to the slide which hosts the chart you want to amend. Double-click the chart. Now double-click the chart component you want to fill. Carry out the following steps:

Ensure this tab is active

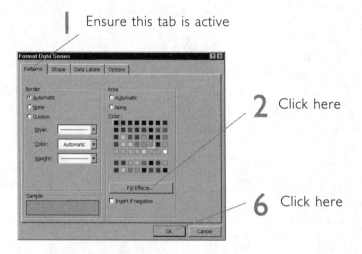

2 Click here

6 Click here

3 Click a tab

REMEMBER

Re step 4 – the available options depend on which tab you've selected in step 3.

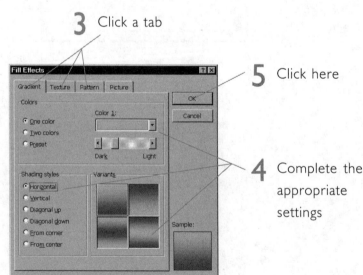

5 Click here

4 Complete the appropriate settings

Formatting chart components (3)

Changing the line width/border style

In Slide view, go to the slide which hosts the chart you want to amend. Double-click the chart. Now double-click the chart component you want to reformat. Carry out step 1 below. Follow 2-3 to apply a line style; 4-5 to apply a line colour; and/or 6-7 to specify a line thickness.

Finally, perform step 8:

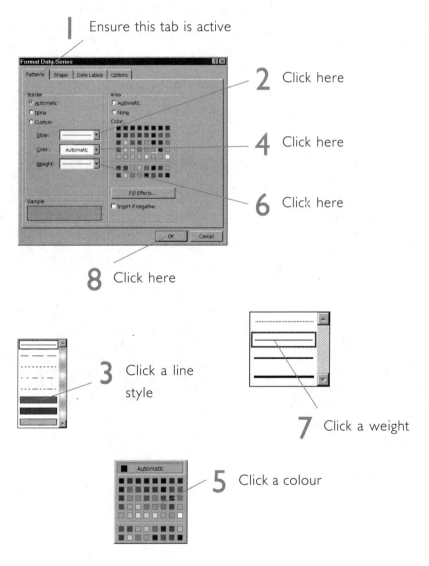

1 Ensure this tab is active

2 Click here

4 Click here

6 Click here

8 Click here

3 Click a line style

7 Click a weight

5 Click a colour

Formatting chart components (4)

To align text, don't carry out step 1 below. Instead, activate the Alignment tab. Select a horizontal and/or vertical alignment. Finally, follow step 4.

Applying a typeface/type size

In Slide view, go to the slide which hosts the chart you want to amend. Double-click the chart. Now double-click the relevant textual component (but see the illustration below).

Double-click here on text objects (not *inside* the frame)

Carry out the following steps:

You can also embolden and/or italicise text.
Click one of the options here before you carry out step 4.

Ensure this tab is active

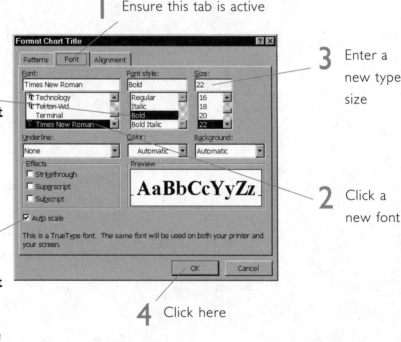

3 Enter a new type size

2 Click a new font

4 Click here

Deselect this if you don't want text resized proportionately when you resize the object to which it is attached.

Working with multimedia

Use this section to learn how to insert clip art and pictures into slides. In the course of doing this, you'll learn about the various graphics formats (bitmap and vector) which PowerPoint recognises and translates, and you'll rescale, crop and recolour images. You'll also discover how to insert sound and film clips into slides, and how to download clips directly from the World Wide Web.

Covers

Multimedia – an overview

PowerPoint lets you enhance presentations in a variety of ways. You can add:

You can add clip art with the use of slide placeholders – see page 105.

- clip art

- third-party pictures

- music or sound clips

- video clips

Once you've inserted clip art and pictures, you can also animate them.

You can animate any slide objects (including text) – see page 114.

You can import sound clips, video clips and clip art via the Clip Gallery. This is a computerised scrapbook which helps you access (and organise) multimedia files. You don't have to use the Clip Gallery to insert these into slides, but it does make the process much easier and more convenient.

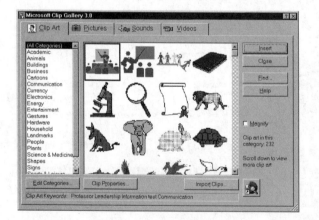

The Clip Gallery

You can also add third-party pictures to your slides. These can be:

- output from other programs (e.g. drawings and illustrations)

- commercial clip art

- photographs

Inserting clip art (1)

If the Clip Gallery *isn't* currently installed on your computer, you'll need to re-run the original installation program to rectify this.

If the Office Clip Gallery is installed on your computer, you can use it to insert clip art. However, you may need to import the relevant images into the Gallery first...

Importing clip art into the Clip Gallery

In Slide or Notes Page view, pull down the Insert menu and click Picture, Clip Art. Now carry out the following steps:

Re step 3 – here we're importing POPULAR.CAG, a relatively brief selection of clip art images copied to your hard disk during installation. POPULAR.CAG is located in the following folder:

msoffice\clipart\pcsfiles

1 Click here

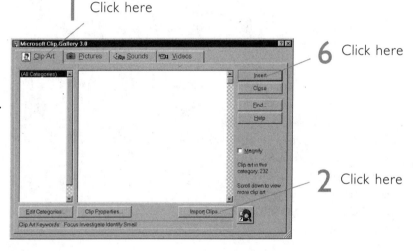

6 Click here

2 Click here

3 Click here; in the list, click the appropriate drive/ folder – see the Remember tip

If you installed PowerPoint from the Office CD, you'll find additional clip art files in the CLIPART folder.

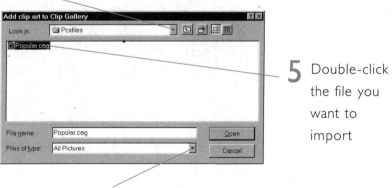

5 Double-click the file you want to import

4 Click here; select All Pictures in the list

Inserting clip art (2)

Adding clip art to slides

In Slide or Notes Page view, go to the slide into which you want the clip art added. Pull down the Insert menu and click Picture, Clip Art. Now carry out the following steps:

Activate the Clip Art tab

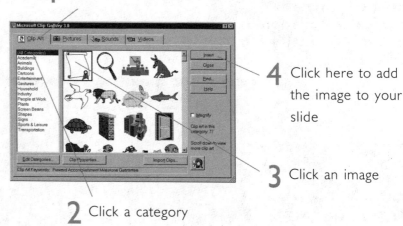

4 Click here to add the image to your slide

3 Click an image

To have clip art appear on every slide, insert it into the Slide master. To have it appear on title slides, insert it into the Title Master.

See Section 3 for how to use the Slide and Title masters.

2 Click a category

A slide with an added clip art image:

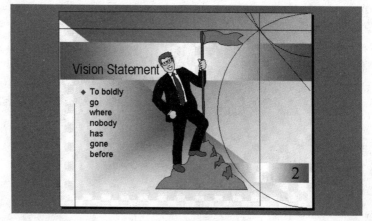

Inserting clip art (3)

You can also import clip art into the Clip Gallery via the World Wide Web, as long as you have:
• **a modem**
• **a live Internet connection**
First launch your Internet browser. Then click this button:

in the Clip Gallery. Do the following:

Click here

Your browser now displays Microsoft's on-line Gallery site. Follow the on-screen instructions to download any relevant clips.

Re step 3 – if you want all available clip art to display, click (All Categories).

Providing the relevant slide has an associated AutoLayout which incorporates a clip art placeholder, you can use this to make inserting an image even easier.

Adding clip art via placeholders

In Slide or Notes Page view, go to the slide into which you want the clip art added. Carry out the following:

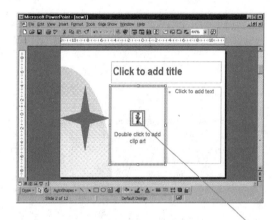

Double-click here

2 Activate the Clip Art tab

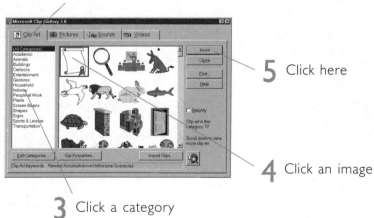

5 Click here

4 Click an image

3 Click a category

Working with the Clip Gallery (1)

In pages 106-108, the term 'clip' refers equally to:
- **clip art**
- **sound clips**
- **movie clips**
(See pages 115-116 for how to use sound and video clips.)

You can also use the Clip Gallery to:

- delete clips

- allocate keywords to clips

- search for specific clips by keywords

- search for specific clips by name and/or suffix

Deleting clips
Launch the Clip Gallery, then do the following:

Activate the relevant tab

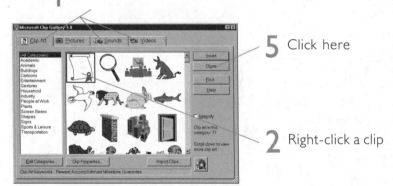

5 Click here

2 Right-click a clip

Deleting a clip only removes the icon which appears in the Clip Gallery; the underlying file still remains on your hard disk (or on the Office CD, if appropriate).

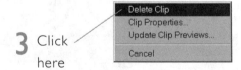

3 Click here

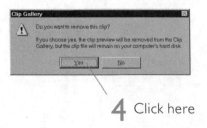

4 Click here

Working with the Clip Gallery (2)

You can allocate 'keywords' to clips, or change existing keyword entries (clips supplied with PowerPoint already have keywords associated with them). This provides a very useful method for cataloguing and retrieving clips.

HANDY TIP

To amend *existing* **keyword entries, follow steps 1-3. In step 4, amend the current keywords as necessary. Then follow steps 5-6.**

Allocating keywords to clips

Launch the Clip Gallery, then do the following:

Activate the relevant tab

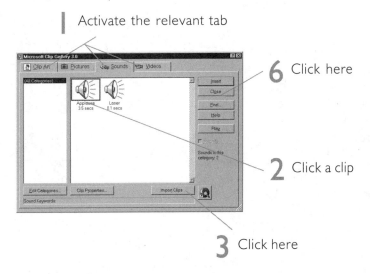

6 Click here

2 Click a clip

3 Click here

4 Type in keywords

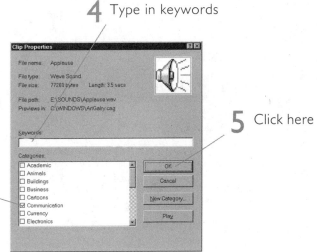

5 Click here

HANDY TIP

To allocate a clip to one or more specific categories, click them here then carry out step 5.

Working with the Clip Gallery (3)

Searching for clips

Launch the Clip Gallery, then do the following:

Activate the relevant tab

5 Click here

2 Click here

HANDY TIP

You can also apply other search parameters. You can search for:

- **files with specific names**
- **files with specific suffixes**

To apply name restrictions, type in the name here:

To find only a specific type, click here and select it from the list:

Finally, follow step 5.

3 Type in search keywords

4 Click here

PowerPoint now displays the first matching clip (if any). To see more, click a different tab in the Clip Gallery. To close the Gallery (if you don't insert any of the clips), press Esc.

Inserting pictures – an overview

Pictures PowerPoint can import into slides fall into two overall categories:

- bitmap images
- vector images

The following are brief details of each (note particularly that there is a certain level of crossover between the two formats):

Bitmap images

Bitmaps consist of pixels (dots) arranged in such a way that they form a graphic image. Because of the very nature of bitmaps, the question of 'resolution' – the sharpness of an image expressed in dpi (dots per inch) – is very important. Bitmaps look best if they're displayed at their correct resolution. You should bear this in mind if you're exporting files from other programs for inclusion in PowerPoint slides.

PowerPoint imports (i.e. translates into its own format) a wide variety of third-party bitmap formats.

See pages 110-111 for more information.

Vector images

PowerPoint will also import vector graphics files in formats native to other programs. Vector images consist of, and are defined by, algebraic equations. One practical result of this is that they can be rescaled without any loss of definition. Another corollary is that they're less complex than bitmaps: they contain less detail.

Vector files can also include bitmap information. For example, PostScript files often have an illustrative header (used for preview purposes) which is a bitmap. This header is very often considerably inferior in quality when compared to the underlying picture.

Picture formats (1)

PowerPoint will happily import a wide selection of bitmap and vector graphic formats. These are some of the main formats:

Many bitmap formats have compression as an option. This allows bitmaps – often very large – to be stored on disk in much smaller files.

Bitmap formats

PCX
An old standby. Originated with PC Paintbrush, a paint program. Used for years to transfer graphics data between Windows applications. Supports compression.

TIFF
Tagged Image File Format. Suffix: .TIF. If anything, even more widely used than PCX, across a whole range of platforms and applications. Supports numerous types and levels of compression.

BMP
Not as common as PCX and TIFF, but still popular. One drawback: sometimes, compression isn't available. It is, however, with PowerPoint.

TGA
Targa. A high-end format, and also a bridge with so-called low-end computers (e.g. Amiga and Atari). Often used in PC and Mac paint and ray-tracing programs because of its high-resolution colour fidelity. Supports compression.

GIF
Graphics Interchange Format. Developed for the on-line transmission of graphics data across the CompuServe network. Just about any Windows program – and a lot more besides – will read GIF. Disadvantage: it can't handle more than 256 colours. One of the few graphics formats which can be used in HTML (HyperText Markup Language) documents on the World Wide Web. Compression is supported.

Picture formats (2)

PCD   (Kodak) PhotoCD. Used primarily to store photographs on CD. Corel Corporation sells a vast range of images in this format.

JPEG   Joint Photographic Experts Group. Suffix: .JPG. Used on the PC and Mac for the storage and display of photographs. One of the few graphics formats which can be used in HTML (HyperText Markup Language) documents on the World Wide Web. Very high levels of compression are built into the format.

Vector formats

CGM   Computer Graphics Metafile. Frequently used in the past, especially as a medium for clip-art transmission. Less frequently used nowadays.

EPS   Encapsulated PostScript. Perhaps the most widely used PostScript format. Actually, PostScript (a programming language in its own right) combines vector *and* bitmap data very successfully. Incorporates a low-resolution bitmap 'header' for preview purposes. If you want to export to a vector format and have a choice, you'd be well advised to use EPS.

WMF   Windows Metafile. Similar to CGM, but even more frequently used. Used for information exchange between just about all Windows programs. Often produces files which are much smaller than the equivalent bitmaps (though not because of compression – there isn't any). If you need a vector format and can't use EPS, use WMF wherever possible.

WPG   Corel WordPerfect's native format. Exists in two flavours.

Inserting pictures

Adding pictures

In Slide or Notes Page view, go to the slide into which you want the picture added. Pull down the Insert menu and do the following:

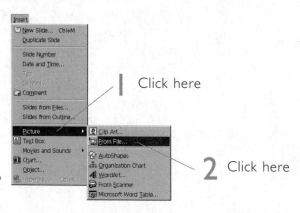

Click here

2 Click here

HANDY TIP

To have clip art appear on every slide, insert it into the Slide master. To have it appear on title slides, insert it into the Title Master.

See Section 3 for how to use the Slide and Title masters.

4 Click here. In the drop-down list, click the drive/folder that hosts the picture

6 Click here

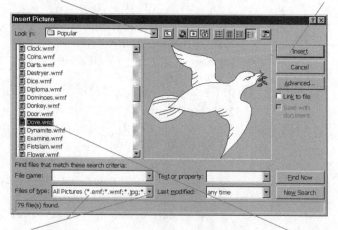

3 Make sure All Pictures is shown. If it isn't, click the arrow and select it from the drop-down list

5 Click the picture file

Working with clip art/pictures (1)

You can perform the following actions on imported clip art and pictures:

- resizing/cropping

- recolouring

You can't recolour imported bitmaps within PowerPoint.

Resizing clip art/pictures

In Slide or Notes Pages view, select the clip art/picture. Now do the following:

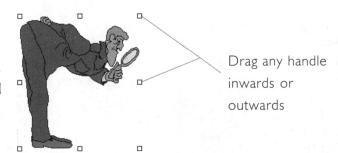

Drag any handle inwards or outwards

If the Picture toolbar isn't currently on-screen, pull down the View menu and click Toolbars, Picture.

Cropping clip art/pictures

In Slide or Notes Pages view, select the clip art/picture. Now refer to the Picture toolbar and do the following:

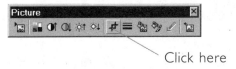

Click here

You can also use the Picture toolbar to adjust image brightness and/or contrast.
 Select the image. Click this button in the toolbar:

 In the Format Picture dialog, activate the Picture tab. Drag the Brightness and Contrast sliders, as appropriate. Click OK.

Move the mouse pointer over any of the image handles and drag it in to crop. Release the mouse button:

Before...

After

Working with clip art/pictures (2)

 REMEMBER

If the Picture toolbar isn't currently on-screen, pull down the View menu and click Toolbars, Picture.

Recolouring clip art/pictures

In Slide or Notes Pages view, select the clip art/picture. Now refer to the Picture toolbar and do the following:

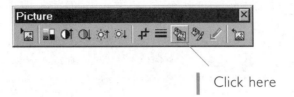

Click here

 HANDY TIP

You can also animate clip art and pictures.
Pull down the Slide Show menu and click Custom Animation. In the Animation order field in the Custom Animation dialog, click an image. Click the arrow to the right of the Entry animation field:

2 Click a colour

5 Click here

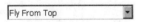

Fly From Top

In the list, select an animation type. Click the Preview button if you want to see what the effect looks like. Finally, click OK.

3 Click the associated arrow

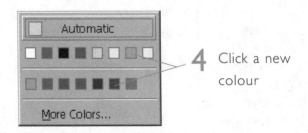

4 Click a new colour

Inserting sound clips

HANDY TIP

To insert more sound clips into the Gallery, follow steps 2-6 on page 103. (In step 2, however, choose Sounds in the drop-down list.)

HANDY TIP

To preview the sound clip before you insert it into your slide, click the Play button. Finally, follow step 2.

BEWARE

You must have a sound card installed in your PC to play back sound clips.

REMEMBER

You can also insert sound clips from file. Pull down the Insert menu and click Movies and Sounds, Sound from File. In the Insert Sound dialog, locate and click a sound file. Click OK.

Sound clips can enhance slide impact tremendously.

Adding sound clips to slides

In Slide view, go to the slide into which you want to insert the sound clip. Now pull down the Insert menu and click Movies and Sounds, Sound from Gallery. Carry out the following steps:

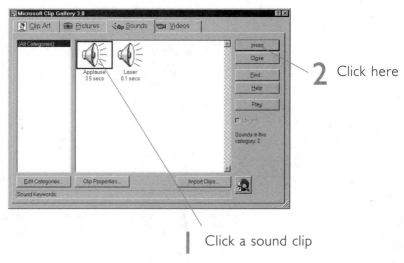

2 Click here

Click a sound clip

Playing a sound clip

In Slide view, go to the relevant slide. Now do the following:

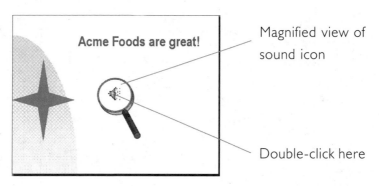

Magnified view of sound icon

Double-click here

Inserting video clips

To insert more video clips into the Gallery, follow steps 2-6 on page 103. (In step 2, however, choose Videos in the drop-down list.)

Video clips can introduce a welcome note of animation into slides.

Adding video clips to slides

In Slide view, go to the slide into which you want to insert the video clip. Now pull down the Insert menu and click Movies and Sounds, Movie from Gallery. Carry out the following steps:

To preview the video clip before you insert it into your slide, click the Play button. The clip runs in a special window:

Finally, follow step 2.

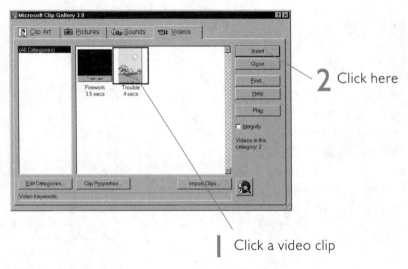

2 Click here

Click a video clip

You can also insert video clips from file. Pull down the Insert menu and click Movies and Sounds, Movie from File. In the Insert Movie dialog, locate and click a film file. Click OK.

Playing a video clip

In Slide view, go to the relevant slide. Now do the following:

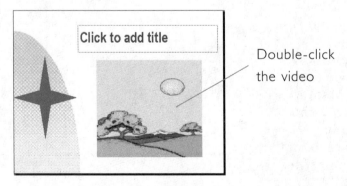

Double-click the video

Finalising the slide show

Use this section to fine-tune your presentation before you get ready to run it. You'll do this by adding summary slides, comments and speaker notes, and by creating handouts, both within PowerPoint itself and also within Microsoft Word (because of its greater formatting capabilities). You'll apply the correct page setup parameters to your slide show, then print it out for proofing purposes. Finally, you'll export slides to third-party formats.

Covers

Fine-tuning your slide show

When you've finished developing your presentation (using the techniques discussed in earlier sections), you should consider adding some last minute enhancements before you prepare it to be run. You can:

Summary slides list the main sections in your presentation for ease of access.

For how to create summary slides, see the Remember tips on page 40. For how to insert hyperlinks (to make the summary slide even more useful), see Section 8.

- create summary s lides (see the Remember tip on the left

- insert internal comments

- add speaker notes

- create handouts

Internal comments aid the review/correction process by allowing presentations to be annotated by multiple users.

Speaker notes are a 'script' which you can create in Notes Page view to help you give the presentation. Many PowerPoint users find these scripts very useful, even indispensable.

Handouts, on the other hand, are printed material which you supply to the slide show audience. Handouts consist of the following:

- an outline which the audience can follow as you speak

- copies of the individual slides (printed one or more to the page)

Additional preparations include:

- specifying page setup parameters

- printing out a proof copy of the presentation

- exporting slides to Word or other formats

Comments – an overview

If your presentation requires to be reviewed, you can insert the necessary comments into the relevant slides. When you've done this, other users can review your annotations, as appropriate. Alternatively, you can simply insert comments for your own information. For example, if you're not sure about the design of a particular slide but want to move on to the next, you could insert a comment (for your own attention) as a reminder that you need to go back to the original slide and review it later...

PowerPoint comments are self-formatting, self-wrapping text boxes:

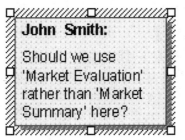

Selected comment

As the above illustration makes clear, when you create a comment, PowerPoint automatically inserts your name – in bold – at the start. When you type in the comment text, the box wraps around the text.

Fine-tuning comments

When you've inserted comments, you can:

- resize them

- view/hide them

- delete them if they've been actioned and are no longer required

- apply any formatting enhancements you want

Inserting a comment

In Slide view, go to the slide into which you want to insert the comment. Pull down the Insert menu and do the following:

Click here

REMEMBER

When you carry out step 1, all comments previously inserted into the current slide become visible.

PowerPoint inserts a new comment, complete with your name as the author. Do the following:

Magnified view of comment box

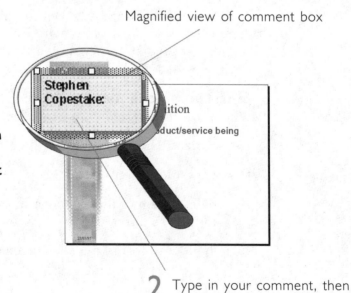

HANDY TIP

To resize a comment box, select it. Then use standard Windows resizing techniques.

2 Type in your comment, then click outside the comment box

Working with comments

Viewing/hiding comments

To make comments visible or invisible (depending on the current setting), refer to the Reviewing toolbar and do the following:

If the Reviewing toolbar isn't currently on-screen, pull down the View menu and click Toolbars, Reviewing.

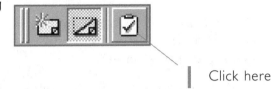

Click here

Note, however, that when you carry out step 1, the effects are global: all slides within the current slide show are affected.

Deleting comments

Ensure comments are currently visible (see above for how to do this). Select the comment you want to erase. Then carry out the following:

To reformat a comment, right-click it. In the menu, click Format Comment. Complete the Format Comment dialog as appropriate. Finally, click OK.

Click anywhere on the comment frame

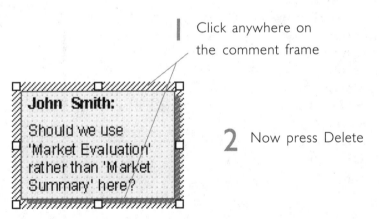

> **John Smith:**
>
> Should we use 'Market Evaluation' rather than 'Market Summary' here?

2 Now press Delete

PowerPoint deletes the comment straight away, without launching a warning message first.

Working with speaker notes (1)

Every PowerPoint slide has a corresponding Notes page which displays:

- a reduced-size version of the slide

- a notes section complete with a notes placeholder

You can use the placeholder to enter notes which you'll refer to (either on-screen or from a printed copy) as you give your presentation.

You can create notes in the following ways:

- from within Notes Page view

- from within Slide view (in a special note editor)

Adding speaker notes within Notes Page view

If you're not already using Notes Page view, pull down the View menu and click Notes Page. Go to the slide into which you want to enter notes. Now do the following:

If you have trouble working with note placeholders, try increasing the Zoom size.
Pull down the View menu and click Zoom. Click a higher zoom %. Click OK.

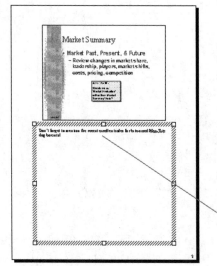

Click in the placeholder. Type in your notes. Then click outside the placeholder.

Working with speaker notes (2)

Adding speaker notes within Slide view

If you're not already using Slide view, pull down the View menu and click Slide. Go to the slide into which you want to enter notes. Pull down the View menu and do the following:

Click here

If you want to add text or pictures to *all* notes pages, add them to the Notes master.
Pull down the View menu and click Master, Notes Master. Click in the note placeholder; add the relevant text and/or picture in the normal way. Finally, carry out the following:

Click here

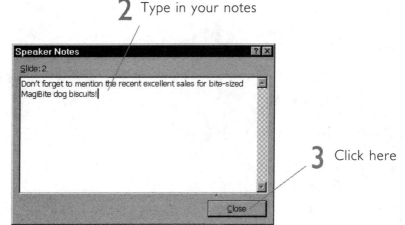

2 Type in your notes

3 Click here

Handouts

You create handouts with the help of the Handouts master.

Creating a handout

Pull down the View menu and do the following:

 HANDY TIP **You can specify the number of slides per page.**
Refer to the Handout Master toolbar and click any of the following:

3 slides   6 slides

2 slides

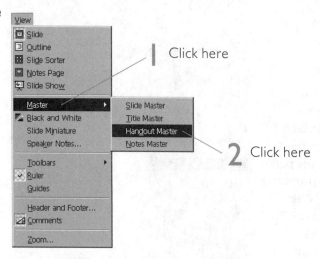

Click here

2 Click here

PowerPoint now launches the Handouts master:

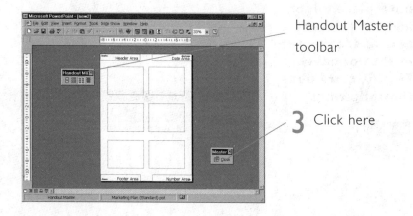

Handout Master toolbar

3 Click here

 HANDY TIP **You can add a header, footer, date and/or page numbering to the handouts.**
Pull down the View menu and click Header and Footer. Complete the Notes and Handouts tab of the Header and Footer dialog as necessary. Finally, click Apply to All.

Use the Header and Footer dialog – see the tip – to customise this as necessary. Finally, follow step 3.

See pages 128-129 for how to print handouts.

See pages 125-126 for how to create handouts in Word.

Exporting handouts to Word (1)

If the procedures listed on page 124 aren't adequate (for instance, if the presentation you're developing also involves a manual), you can create your handout in Word. When you do this, PowerPoint transfers all notes/slides automatically while letting you choose the handout format. You can then use the greater formatting capabilities innate in Word to produce the handout you need.

Exporting to Word

Pull down the File menu and carry out the following steps:

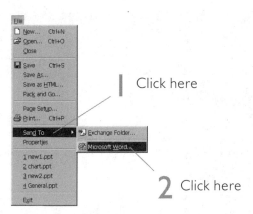

1 Click here

2 Click here

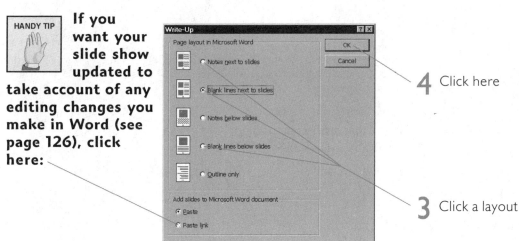

HANDY TIP

If you want your slide show updated to take account of any editing changes you make in Word (see page 126), click here:

4 Click here

3 Click a layout

Exporting handouts to Word (2)

PowerPoint now starts Word (if it isn't already running) and:

- creates a new document

- inserts your presentation (with the requested layout) into the new document

Do the following:

 REMEMBER

If you need help with using Word, consider buying a companion volume: Word in easy steps

or

Word 97 in easy steps

For how to order it, see the front of this book.

The inserted presentation – edit and save this in the normal way

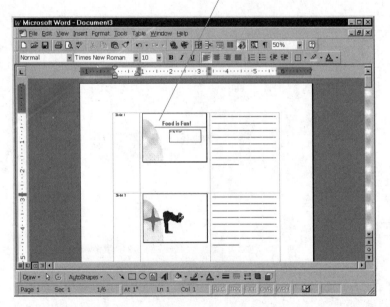

If you clicked "Paste link" on page 125 (see the Handy Tip), any editing changes you make in Word are automatically reflected in your original presentation.

Page setup issues

Before you print a slide show, it's a good idea to specify:

- whether you want to print slides in Landscape (the default) or Portrait format

- the dimensions of the printed page

There are two aspects to every page size: a vertical measurement and a horizontal measurement. These can be varied according to orientation. There are two possible orientations:

Portrait   Landscape

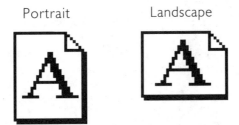

Specifying page setup options
Pull down the File menu and click Page Setup. Now do the following:

HANDY TIP **You can specify the start point from which slides are numbered. Type in the start number here:**

Click here; select a slide size in the list

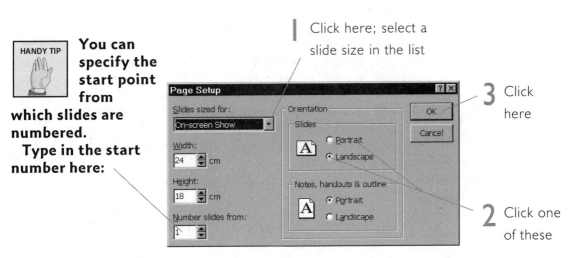

3 Click here

2 Click one of these

Printing your slide show (1)

You can print any presentation component. These include:

- slides

- notes

- outlines

- handouts

- comments

You can also:

 To print internal comments, simply ensure that they're currently visible. See page 121 for how to do this.

- specify the number of copies

- specify slide ranges (e.g. slides 1-6 inclusive and 11)

- customise your printer's setup

- have printed copies collated

- print out slides in greyscale, or black-and-white

- proportionately scale printed output up or down to match your paper size

Alternatively, you can simply opt to print your presentation with the default options in force (PowerPoint provides a 'fast track' approach to this).

Collation

Collation is the process whereby PowerPoint prints one full copy of a presentation at a time. For instance, if you're printing three copies of a 25-slide presentation, PowerPoint prints slides 1-25 of the first slide show, followed by slides 1-25 of the second and slides 1-25 of the third.

Collation is only possible if you're printing multiple copies of a slide show.

Printing your slide show (2)

Ensure Collate is selected if you want output collated.

Click "Scale to fit paper" to have output scaled evenly to fit your paper size.

Ensure Black & white is selected if you want to print out in greyscale. Click Pure black & white to print out in mono.

Re step 43 – separate non-adjacent slides with commas – e.g. to print slides 5, 12 & 16 type in: '5,12,16'. Enter contiguous slides with dashes – e.g. to print slides 12 to 23 inclusive, type: '12-23'. (Omit the quote marks in all examples.)

Printing a presentation

Pull down the File menu and click Print. Now carry out any of steps 1-5 below, as appropriate. Finally, follow step 6.

1 Click here; select the printer you want from the list

2 Click here to print the current slide only

3 Type in the number of copies required

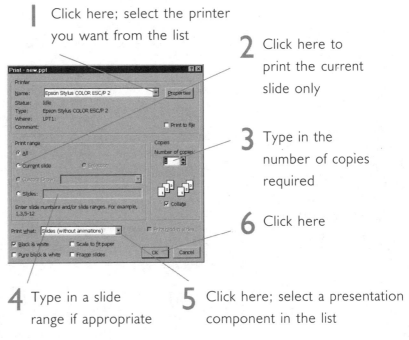

6 Click here

4 Type in a slide range if appropriate

5 Click here; select a presentation component in the list

Customising printer setup

Click the Properties button:

Properties

in the Print dialog. Then complete the resultant dialogs (for how to do this, see your printer's manual). Finally, complete step 6 above.

Fast-track printing

To print using all the default settings, without launching the Print dialog, simply click the Print button on the Standard toolbar:

Exporting slide shows/slides

It's sometimes useful to be able to export the following:

- entire presentations

- individual slides

to third-party formats. For example, you may want to export the whole of a slide show to:

- an earlier version of PowerPoint, so you can work with it on a different machine

- a RTF outline, which allows your presentation to be read by many different software programs

See pages 110-111 for broad details of bitmap and vector graphics formats.

Alternatively, you may wish to export one slide (or all slides within a presentation) as a picture, for example in GIF format.

Exporting slides

Pull down the File menu and click Save As. Carry out the following steps:

2 Click here. In the drop-down list, click the drive you want to host the exported file

Re step 1 – if you select a graphics format, e.g.:
- **GIF (Graphics Interchange Format)**
- **JPEG**
each slide – unless you specify otherwise – is saved as a separate picture file.

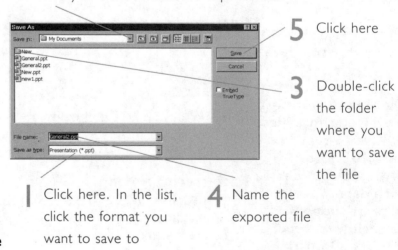

5 Click here

3 Double-click the folder where you want to save the file

1 Click here. In the list, click the format you want to save to

4 Name the exported file

Preparing slide shows

Use this section to prepare your presentation to be run. This involves applying transitions (the process of determining how adjacent slides supersede each other); animations (special effects applied to individual slide objects); and hyperlinks (buttons which jump to specific slides or locations). You'll also stipulate the length of time each slide is on-screen. Finally, you'll create a custom slide show (for a specific audience) and ensure your presentation is set up correctly.

Covers

Preparation – an overview

PowerPoint provides a wide assortment of techniques you can use to ensure that your presentation has the maximum impact. These are all ways of preparing your slide show for its eventual performance.

 See Section 9 for how to perform – 'run' – slide shows.

You can:

- specify *transitions* (interactions between individual slides)

- apply *animations* (used to control how each slide element is introduced to the audience)

- insert *hyperlinks* (buttons which – when clicked – jump to additional slides)

- customise slide timings (the intervals between individual slides)

- customise the presentations setup

Presentation setup

Presentation setup specifies:

- which slides do or do not display. Use this to prepare presentations which are tailored for specific audiences (some slides may not be suitable for a given recipient)

- the type of slide show delivery. You can determine whether presentations run normally (i.e. orchestrated by the presenter), in a special window or at a conference kiosk

- whether the presentation runs in 'loop' mode

- whether slides are advanced manually, or using the preset timings

Transitions (1)

Transitions add visual interest to presentations by customising the crossover between individual slides. PowerPoint provides 41 separate transition effects. These include:

Random Transition	PowerPoint selects and applies the transition
Blinds Horizontal or Vertical	The next slide displays like a blind
Checkerboard Across or Down	The next slide displays with a chequered pattern
Box In or Out	The next slide displays as an increasing or decreasing box

When you apply a transition to a specific slide, the effect takes place between the previous and selected slides.

You can specify transitions effects:

- on all slides within a presentation

- on individual slides

Applying transitions en masse
In any view, pull down the Slide Show menu and do the following:

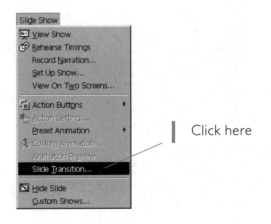

Click here

Transitions (2)

Now carry out the following steps:

Click here

3 Click here

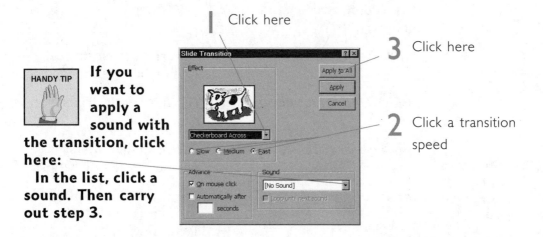

HANDY TIP
If you want to apply a sound with the transition, click here:
In the list, click a sound. Then carry out step 3.

2 Click a transition speed

HANDY TIP
If you're not currently in Slide Sorter view, pull down the View menu and click Slide Sorter.

Applying transitions singly
In Slide Sorter view, do the following:

2 Click here

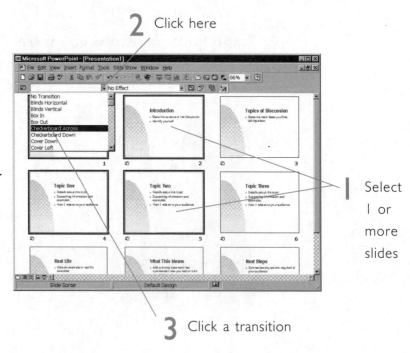

HANDY TIP
Re step 1 – to select more than one slide, hold down Shift as you click the slide icons.

Select 1 or more slides

3 Click a transition

Animations (1)

You can use animations to:

- introduce objects onto a slide one at a time (by default, they all appear on-screen at once)

- apply special effects to objects

Having objects appear in a staggered way maximises slide impact; the eye is drawn to areas of specific interest in a way which makes them more prominent.

Imposing special effects on objects is particularly useful in the following scenarios:

- having individual items in a bulleted list appear one at a time

- having pictures, clip art or charts become prominent slowly

You can apply preset animations (PowerPoint comes with 8) or create your own.

HANDY TIP

You can also apply animations to an entire slide (but you have a wider choice of presets: 12).
In Slide Sorter view, select one or more slides. Then follow steps 1-2.

Applying a preset animation

In Slide view, pull down the Slide Show menu and do the following:

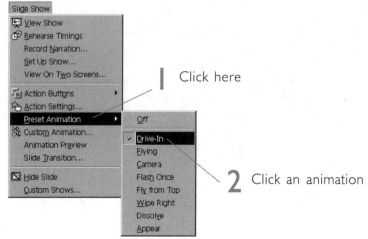

Click here

2 Click an animation

Animations (2)

You can apply special effects to text. For example, you can control how progressively text displays...

Follow steps 1-2. Now complete the Introduce text section, as appropriate. Finally, carry out step 3.

Customising animations

In Slide view, right-click the object you want to animate and do the following:

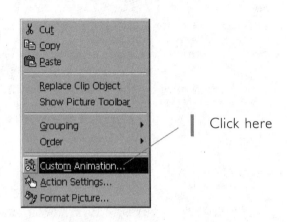

Click here

If you have a sound card fitted (with external speakers) and want to associate a sound with the animation, click here:

Select a sound in the drop-down list. Finally, carry out step 3.

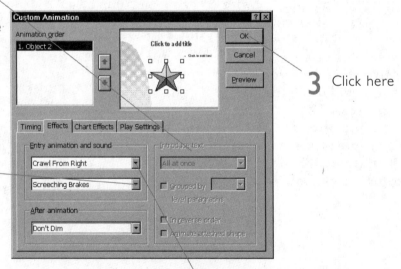

3 Click here

2 Click here; select an animation in the list

Animations (3)

Previewing animations

In Slide view, select the object you want to animate. Pull down the Slide Show menu and do the following:

 Previewing also plays any associated sound tracks.

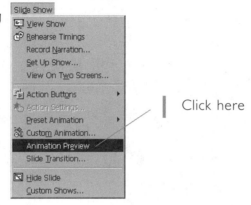

Click here

 When the Animation Preview window launches, it automatically previews the selected object/ animation. If you want to repeat this, simply click anywhere within the window.

PowerPoint now launches the Animation Preview window:

Animation Preview window

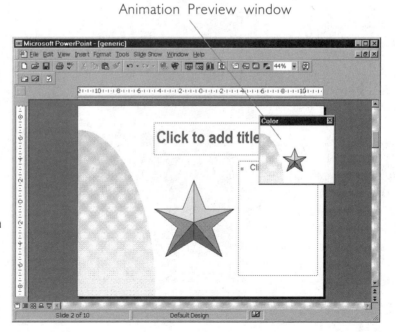

 To close the Animation Preview window, click here: **X** in the upper-right corner.

Hyperlinks (1)

'URL' stands for Uniform Resource Locator. URLs are unique addresses for World Wide Web sites.

If you need more information on the Internet, consider buying 'Internet UK in easy steps'.

You can insert hyperlinks into slides. In PowerPoint, hyperlinks are 'action buttons' which you can click (while a presentation is being run – see Section 9) to jump to a prearranged destination immediately. This can be:

- preset slide targets (for instance, the first, last, next or previous slide)

- a specific slide (where *you* select a slide from a special dialog)

- a URL (providing you have a live Internet connection and an installed modem)

- another PowerPoint presentation

- another file

Inserting an action button

In Slide or Notes Page view, pull down the Slide Show menu. Do the following:

Action buttons are actually AutoShapes. See Section 4 for how to work with AutoShapes.

In particular, carry out the procedures in the first Handy Tip on page 75 to add text which describes the destination (e.g. 'Slide 13').

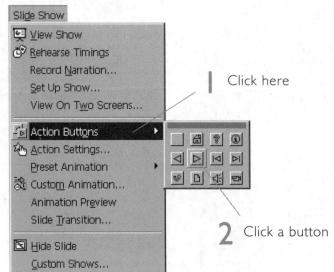

Click here

2 Click a button

Hyperlinks (2)

Now position the mouse pointer at the location on the slide where you want the button inserted. Hold down the left mouse button and drag to define the button. Release the mouse button and carry out the following steps:

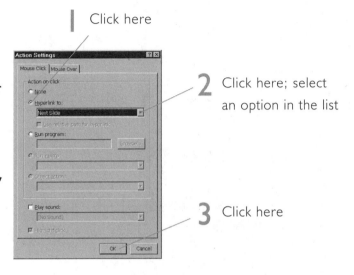

Click here

2 Click here; select an option in the list

3 Click here

where you select a destination slide. Complete the dialog as necessary, then click OK. Finally, carry out step 3.

The illustration below shows an inserted action button/hyperlink:

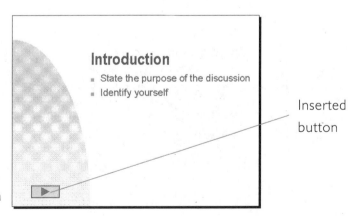

Inserted button

Specifying slide timing (1)

The rehearsal method (a kind of dummy-run) is especially suitable for ensuring that the slide timings you insert are workable.

You can specify how long each slide is on-screen, and by implication the duration of the entire presentation. There are two ways to do this:

- from within Slide Sorter view (either singly, or for every slide)

- by 'rehearsing' the presentation

Applying timings in Slide Sorter view

Select one or more slides, then pull down the Slide Show menu and do the following:

You can follow the procedures here to amend *existing* timings (or to reset them to zero – see the Handy Tip on page 141).

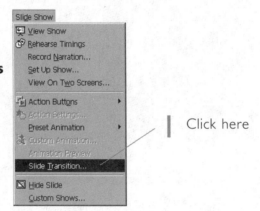

Click here

Re step 3 – click Apply to All to have the timing applied to *every* slide in the show.

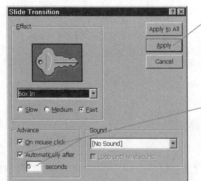

3 Click here to apply the new timings to the selected slide(s)

2 Click here, then type in a slide duration in seconds

Specifying slide timing (2)

Rehearsing slides uses a special PowerPoint feature: the Slide Meter.

Applying timings with the Slide Meter

In any view, pull down the Slide Show menu and do the following:

Click here

PowerPoint launches its rehearsal window, with the first slide (and the Slide Meter) displayed. Do the following:

If you've set any manual timings (using the method discussed under 'Applying timings in Slide Sorter view' on page 140), clear them before you use the rehearsal method. (For how to do this, see the Remember tip on page 140.)

2 This timer counts the interval until the next slide; when the timing is right, follow step 3

3 Click here

After step 3, PowerPoint moves to the next slide. Repeat steps 2 and 3 until all the slides have had intervals allocated. Finally, another message appears. Do the following:

4 Click here

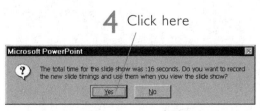

Presentation setup (1)

PowerPoint lets you create custom slide shows. Custom shows allow you to adopt a 'mix and match' approach by selecting specific slides from the active presentation. This allows you to tailor a base slide show for specific audiences and/or occasions.

Creating a custom show

Select one or more slides, then pull down the Slide Sorter menu and do the following:

HANDY TIP

For how to run a custom show, see Section 9.

1 Click here

2 Click here

6 Click here

3 Name the custom show

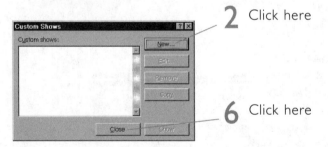

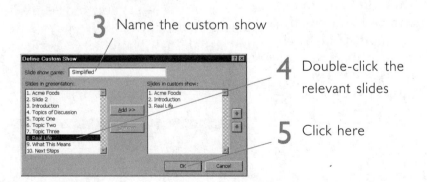

4 Double-click the relevant slides

5 Click here

Presentation setup (2)

Once you've set up a custom slide show, you can:

- remove slides

- add new slides

- move slides up or down

Editing a custom show

Follow step 1 on page 142. Then carry out steps 1-2 below. To add a new slide, follow step 3. To remove a slide, perform steps 4 and 5. To change the slide order, follow step 4, and then 6 OR 7. Finally, carry out step 8.

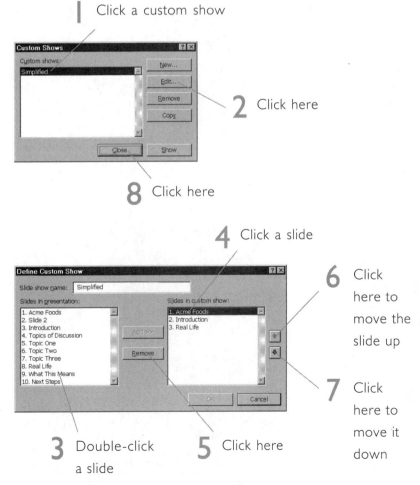

1 Click a custom show

2 Click here

8 Click here

4 Click a slide

6 Click here to move the slide up

7 Click here to move it down

3 Double-click a slide

5 Click here

Presentation setup (3)

The final stage in slide show preparation involves telling PowerPoint:

- the type of presentation you want to run

- whether you want it to run perpetually

- whether you want each slide to appear automatically

Setting up a presentation

Pull down the Slide Show menu and carry out step 1 below. Then carry out any of steps 2-4. Finally, perform step 5.

Click here

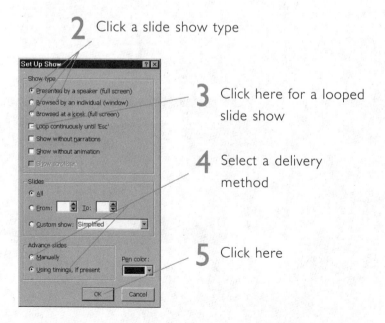

2 Click a slide show type

3 Click here for a looped slide show

4 Select a delivery method

5 Click here

Presenting slide shows

Use this section to learn how to present your slide show to a live audience. You'll discover how to move around in live presentations, and how to accentuate slide areas with the Light Pen. Next you'll save your slide show as a 'run-time' file (so it can be run on machines which don't have PowerPoint installed). You'll also create World Wide Web documents using specific templates and the AutoContent Wizard. Finally, you'll access data directly from the Web, and run PowerPoint Central, Microsoft's on-line PowerPoint magazine.

Covers

Running your presentation

 We've already discussed Web publishing briefly on page 46. Here, we expand on the theme.

 To run a custom slide show, pull down the Slide Show menu and click Custom Show. In the Custom shows field in the Custom Show dialog, click the show you want to run. Click Show.
To stop the show, press Esc.

 Later topics in this section often ask you to right-click in a slide to produce a pop-up menu. You can achieve the same effect by left clicking the pop-up button.

By now, your presentation is ready to run. PowerPoint lets you:

- present it to a live audience (the most common scenario)

- create a run-time file (which enables slide shows to be run on PCs which don't have PowerPoint installed)

- publish your slide show on the World Wide Web

Running your slide show live

Pull down the Slide Show menu and click View Show. PowerPoint launches the first slide in a special window:

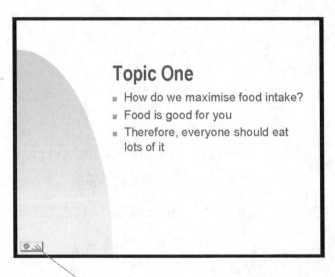

Pop-up button

If, in step 4 on page 144, you selected 'Using timings, if present', PowerPoint displays the next slide automatically. If, on the other hand, you selected 'Manually', you now control when the next slide appears: simply left-click once. Repeat as and when necessary.

For details of other navigational techniques, see page 147.

Navigating through slide shows

For how to use other PowerPoint views, see pages 16-17.

Navigating – the keystroke approach

When you run a presentation, you're actually using a special view called Slide Show. There are special commands you can use to move around in Slide Show view. Press any of the keystrokes listed in the left column to produce the desired result (shown on the right):

Enter or Page Down	Jumps to the next slide
Page Up	Jumps to the previous slide
Home	Jumps to the first slide
End	Jumps to the last slide
'Slide number' and Enter	Jumps to the specified slide

For example, to go to slide 6,

type:
6
then press Enter.

Navigating with the Slide Navigator

You can also use a dialog route to navigate in Slide Show view.

Within Slide Show view, right-click once. In the menu which appears, click Go, Slide Navigator. Do the following:

If you want to view a slide which is in a custom slide show, click here:

In the list, select the custom slide show. Then follow step 1.

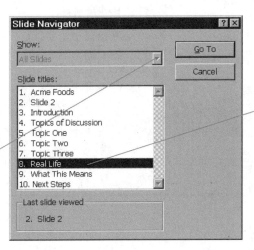

Double-click the slide you want to view

Emphasising slide shows

PowerPoint lets you emphasise slides during a live presentation. You do this by using a feature known as the Light Pen.

Using the Light Pen

In Slide Show view, right-click once. Do the following:

Click here

Marks you make with the Light Pen are only temporary: they disappear when you move to another slide.

The mouse pointer changes to a pen. Position this near the area you want to emphasise and drag to accentuate it:

You can specify the colour used by the Light Pen. Right-click the slide. In the menu, click Pointer Options, Pen Color. In the list, click a colour.

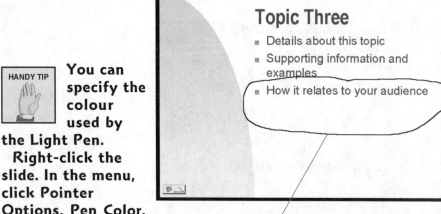

A bulleted point emphasised with the Light Pen

Run-time presentations (1)

If you need to take a slide show to an audience, you can have PowerPoint create a compressed – 'run-time' – file (occupying more than one floppy disk, if necessary) containing:

- the active presentation

- ancillary information (e.g. typeface details)

- a minimal PowerPoint viewer (a small program which enables PCs which lack PowerPoint to run presentations)

PowerPoint uses a special wizard to create run-time files.

Using the Pack and Go Wizard

In any view, pull down the File menu and click Pack and Go. Carry out the following steps:

REMEMBER **Run-time files don't *have* to contain typeface data or the PowerPoint viewer: these are optional, though often desirable.**

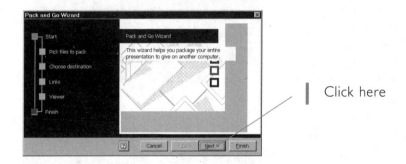

| Click here

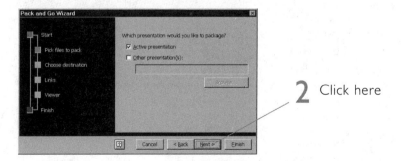

2 Click here

Run-time presentations (2)

Re step 3 – select Embed TrueType Fonts if your slide show uses typefaces which are unlikely to be on the destination PC. This results in a bigger file, but one which is guaranteed to run correctly.

Now perform the following additional steps:

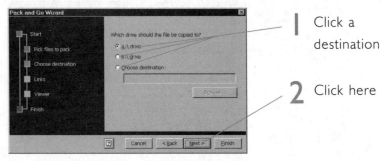

1 Click a destination

2 Click here

To unload your run-time file on the destination PC, launch Explorer. Go to the folder containing the file. Double-click PNGSETUP.EXE. **Follow the on-screen instructions.**

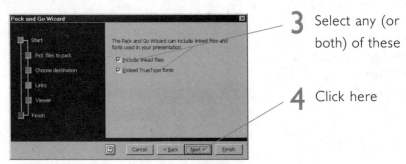

3 Select any (or both) of these

4 Click here

To open the viewer, start Explorer. In the folder which holds your slide show, double-click PPVIEW32.EXE. **Double-click the show in the Look in field.**

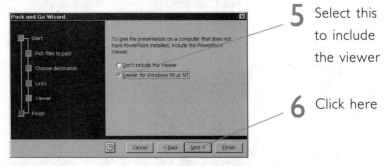

5 Select this to include the viewer

6 Click here

The final Wizard dialog now appears. Click here:

Creating Web pages (1)

In Section 2, we looked at how to create new slide shows with:

- the AutoContent Wizard

- templates

Now we'll explore the creation of presentations which are specifically suitable for use on the World Wide Web.

Creating a Web page with the AutoContent Wizard

Follow steps 1-3 on page 25, then 1-3 on page 26. Now do the following:

See page 46 for how to save *existing* slide shows into HTML format for use on the World Wide Web.

Before you send your HTML files to your Internet provider, open then in a browser – e.g. Internet Explorer – to make sure they display correctly.

If they don't, amend the original presentation appropriately and re-export it to HTML.

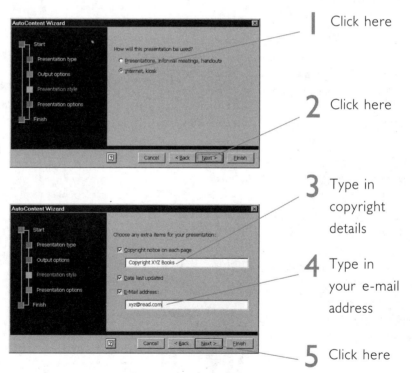

1 Click here

2 Click here

3 Type in copyright details

4 Type in your e-mail address

5 Click here

The final Wizard dialog now appears. Click here:

Creating Web pages (2)

In Section 2, we explored the creation of slide shows based on templates. However, PowerPoint has special templates which can help you create presentations specifically for use on the World Wide Web.

Creating a Home Page based on a template

Pull down the File menu and click New. Then click the Presentations tab. Double-click either of these icons:

Personal Home Page (Online).pot

Corporate Home Page (Online).pot

See page 46 for how to save *existing* **slide shows into HTML format for use on the World Wide Web.**

Edit the presentation appropriately, then save it to disk in HTML format – see the Remember tip. Finally, send it to your Internet provider (but see the Handy Tip first).

Creating Web Page banners based on templates

Pull down the File menu and click New. Click the Web Pages tab. Double-click either of these icons:

Sample Banner1.pot

Sample Banner2.pot

Before you send your HTML files to your Internet provider, open then in a browser – e.g. Internet Explorer – to make sure they display correctly.
If they don't, amend the original presentation appropriately and re-export it to HTML.

Edit the presentation appropriately, then save it to disk in HTML format – see the Remember tip. Finally, send it to your Internet provider (but see the Handy Tip first).

The Corporate Home Page template in action

Accessing data on the Web

You also need to have started your Web browser.

PowerPoint has inbuilt links to dedicated Microsoft World Wide Web pages. Provided you have:

- a modem

- a live connection to an Internet service provider

you can connect almost immediately to:

- an on-line support page

- live Product News

- Frequently Asked Questions

You can also access a section called Free Stuff. Click Free Stuff in the File sub-menu to download free additions to PowerPoint – for instance, extra templates or animations.

Viewing Web data

With a live Internet connection, pull down the Help menu and click Microsoft on the Web. Now click any of the following in the sub-menu:

- Product News

- Frequently Asked Questions

- Online Support

To return to the previously viewed Web screen, press Alt+←.

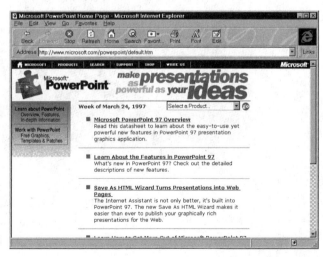

The Product News page in Internet Explorer

To close down your browser at any time, press Alt+F4. Don't forget to terminate your Internet connection, too!

Accessing PowerPoint Central

PowerPoint Central is an on-line magazine containing

- articles and tips for enhanced presentations

- hyperlinks which jump to Internet sites

You can use these hyperlinks (buttons you click to jump to a destination) to achieve access to:

- additional clip art and graphic effects

- videos and sound clips

- templates and tips

Using PowerPoint Central

First, ensure your Internet connection is live and your browser is running. Pull down the Tools menu and click PowerPoint Central. Now do the following:

 HANDY TIP

Before PowerPoint Central launches, the following message appears:

Click Yes to have PowerPoint check whether an update is due.

 HANDY TIP

To return to the previously viewed PowerPoint Central screen, press Alt+←.

 HANDY TIP

To close down your browser at any time, press Alt+F4. Don't forget to terminate your Internet connection, too!

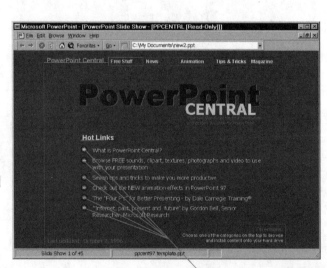

Click any of these to open the appropriate Web page in your browser

Index

S

HANDY REFERENCE

Universal

Ctrl+N .... Creates a new presentation
Ctrl+O .... Opens an existing presentation
Ctrl+W .... Closes a presentation
Ctrl+S .... Saves the active document
Ctrl+P .... Prints the active document
Ctrl+F .... Launches a find operation
Ctrl+H .... Launches a find-and-replace operation
Ctrl+A (in Slide view) .... Selects all objects
    (in Slide Sorter view) .... Selects all slides
    (in Outline view) .... Selects all text
Ctrl+Z .... Undo
Ctrl+Y .... Reverses Undo
Page Up .... Moves to the previous slide
Page Down .... Moves to the next slide
Ctrl+M .... Inserts a new slide (via the New Slide dialog)
F1 .... Launches the Office Assistant

On text

Ctrl+B .:.. Emboldens (or removes emboldening)
Ctrl+I .... Italicises (or removes italicisation)
Ctrl+U .... Underlines (or removes underlining)

When running a slide show

Return or Page Down .... Goes to next slide
Page Up .... Goes to previous slide
F1 .... Launches a list of commands (press Esc to clear)
'Slide number'+Return .... Goes to the specified slide
Ctrl+P .... Launches the Light Pen
Ctrl+A .... Terminates the Light Pen
E .... Erases Light Pen markings
S .... Pauses/restarts an automatic presentation
Esc .... Terminates a slide show

About the Series

In easy steps series is developed for time-sensitive people who want results fast. It is designed for quick, easy and effortless learning. Titles include:

Operating Systems		General	
Psion 5	1-874029-87-3	Design and Typography	1-84078-004-5
Windows 98	1-874029-70-9	Networking	1-874029-92-X
Windows 95	1-874029-28-8	PCs	1-874029-90-3
Windows CE	1-874029-80-6	Upgrading Your PC	1-874029-76-8
Windows NT	1-874029-94-6	**Internet**	
Main Office Applications		AOL UK	1-874029-97-0
Access	1-874029-78-4	CompuServe UK	1-874029-33-4
Excel	1-874029-69-5	FrontPage	1-874029-60-1
Microsoft Office 97	1-874029-66-0	HTML	1-874029-86-5
Microsoft Office	1-874029-37-7	Internet Explorer 4	1-874029-84-9
Microsoft Office SBE	1-874029-81-4	Internet UK	1-874029-73-3
Microsoft Works	1-84078-001-0	MSN UK	1-874029-93-8
PowerPoint	1-874029-63-6	Netscape Communicator	1-874029-98-9
SmartSuite	1-874029-67-9	Web Page Design	1-874029-91-1
Word 97	1-874029-68-7	**Accounting and Finance**	
Word	1-874029-39-3	Microsoft Money UK	1-874029-61-X
WordPerfect	1-874029-59-8	QuickBooks UK	1-874029-83-0
Graphics and Desktop Publishing		Quicken UK	1-874029-71-7
AutoCAD LT	1-84078-005-3	Sage Instant Accounting	1-84078-003-7
CorelDRAW	1-84078-000-2	Sage Sterling for Windows	1-874029-79-2
PageMaker	1-84078-002-9	**Development Tools**	
PagePlus	1-874029-49-0	Delphi	1-874029-96-2
Paint Shop Pro	1-874029-95-4	JavaScript	1-874029-89-X
Photoshop	1-874029-82-2	Visual Basic	1-874029-74-1
Publisher	1-874029-77-6	Visual C++	1-874029-88-1
QuarkXPress	1-874029-99-7	Visual J++	1-874029-75-X

Web: http://www.computerstep.com

Tel: +44 (0)1926 817999   Fax: +44 (0)1926 817005   Email: books@computerstep.com